S0-ATU-888

TROTSKY

David King was born in London in 1943. He studied graphic design at the London College of Printing from 1960 to 1963, has been Art Editor of the *Sunday Times Magazine* since 1965, and has worked as a free-lance designer, photographer and illustrator for many publications. Francis Wyndham was born in London in 1924, has been a literary journalist since 1946, and has written criticism of books, films and plays for innumerable publications. Since 1964 he has also worked as an assistant editor on the *Sunday Times Magazine*.

TROTSKY

a documentary

by Francis Wyndham and David King

Penguin Books / Allen Lane The Penguin Press

Penguin Books Ltd, Harmondsworth, Middlesex, England
Penguin Books Inc., 7110 Ambassador Road, Baltimore, Maryland 21207, U.S.A.
Penguin Books Australia Ltd, Ringwood, Victoria, Australia
Allen Lane The Penguin Press, 74 Grosvenor Street, London W1

Paperback: ISBN 0 14 00.3522 2
Hardback: ISBN 0 7139. 0334 1

First published 1972
Copyright © Francis Wyndham and David King, 1972

Printed in Great Britain by Hazells Offset Ltd, Slough, Bucks
Colour printing and binding by Hazell Watson & Viney Ltd, Aylesbury, Bucks

This book is sold subject to the condition that it shall not,
by way of trade or otherwise, be lent, re-sold, hired out,
or otherwise circulated without the publisher's prior consent
in any form of binding or cover other than that in
which it is published and without a similar condition being
imposed on the subsequent purchaser

TROTSKY

Contents

Conspiracy 1879-1917

Trotsky in his early twenties — 'mug-shots' kept in their files on dangerous revolutionaries by the Secret Police of Imperial Russia

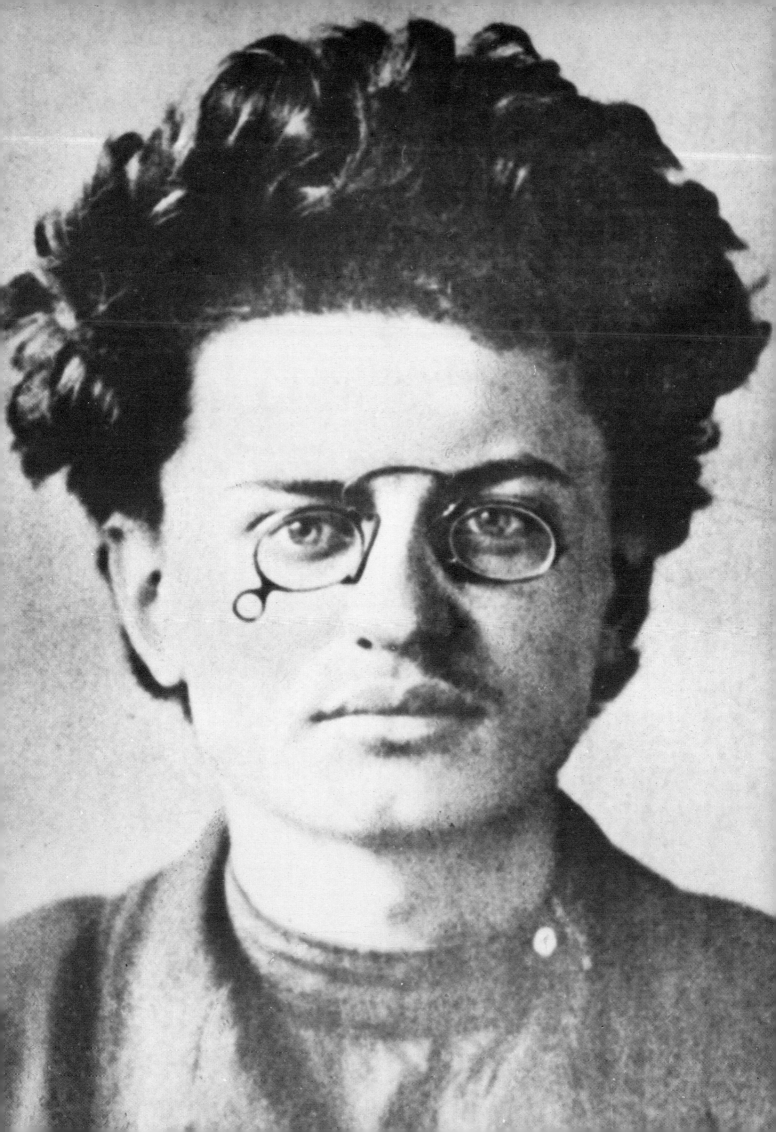

The first nine years of Trotsky's life were spent on an empty, peaceful steppe in the Southern Ukraine, 'a kingdom o
wheat and sheep . . . firmly guarded against the invasion of politics by its great open spaces and the absence of roads'
Here, in the summer of 1879, a Jewish farmer had moved with his family to a lonely village called Yanovka, near the smal
town of Bobrinetz in the province of Kherson. David Leontievich Bronstein was then a tough, illiterate countryman o

bout thirty, ambitious to improve his material lot by hard physical labour – at first his own and later, as he grew more
rosperous, that of others. When they arrived at Yanovka – a mud hut thatched with straw, some crude farm buildings
nd nearly seven hundred acres of land – his wife Anna was expecting her fifth child; and on 26 October she gave birth to a
on, Lev Davidovich. On the same day of the same month thirty-eight years later, this boy (under the name of Leon

Trotsky) was to lead the Bolshevik insurrection with Lenin and change the face of the world.

The 1870s in Russia had witnessed the rise of the Narodniks, or Populist movement. Calling their organization 'Land and Freedom', a handful of idealistic intellectuals had undertaken to educate the peasants by living among them and distributing tracts on the evils of Tsarism. In 1879, this peaceful phase having proved abortive, a split occurred in the movement and a new group was formed around the slogan 'Freedom for the People', dedicated to bringing about the downfall of autocratic rule by individual acts of terrorism. The year of Trotsky's birth was also the date of the first assaults on Tsarism by dynamite – a desperate tactic which reached its climax two years later with the assassination of Alexander II. But this coup only brought a second disillusion; it evoked no response from the oppressed peasantry, which remained as suspicious of the terrorist wing among the Populists as it had been of their purely propagandist efforts. The new Tsar, Alexander III, came in on a wave of outraged reaction and anti-liberal legislation, and throughout the 1880s and the early 1890s revolutionary activity in Russia was at its lowest ebb. It is thus not surprising that the young Trotsky – future prophet of Permanent Revolution – should have remained aloof from politics for seventeen years. The early chapters of his autobiography *My Life*, written in 1929, describe his childhood at home with a calm beauty, a sense of limitless space and time combined with a loving attention to minute detail, that derive from the great tradition of the nineteenth-century Russian novel.

'My father and mother lived out their hard-working lives with some friction, but very happily on the whole. My mother came from a family of townspeople who looked down on farmers, with their rough hands. But my father had been handsome and graceful in his youth, with a manly, energetic face . . . Of the eight children born of this marriage, four . . . died in infancy, of diphtheria and scarlet fever, deaths almost as unnoticed as was the life of those who survived. The land, the cattle, the poultry, the mill, took all my parents' time; there was none left for us. The seasons succeeded one another, and waves of farm work swept over domestic affection. There was no display of tenderness in my family, especially during my early years, but there was a strong comradeship of labour between my father and mother.

'"Give your mother a chair!" my father would cry as soon as my mother crossed the threshold, white with dust from the mill. "Mashka! Light the samovar, quick!" my mother would command even before she had reached the house. "Your master will soon be in from the fields." Both knew what it was to have reached the limit of physical exhaustion.

'My father was undoubtedly superior to my mother, both in intellect and character. He was deeper, more reserved, more tactful. He . . . never made a mistake in what he bought: cloth, hats, shoes, horses or machinery, he always got his money's worth. "I don't like money," he once said to me later, as if apologizing for being so mean, "but I like it less when there is none of it . . ."

'My mother loved to read during the long winters, when Yanovka was swept by the snow drifting from all the corners of the steppe and rising over the windows. She would sit on a small three-cornered seat in the dining-room with her feet on a chair before her, or, when the early winter twilight fell, she would move into my father's armchair near the small, frosty window, and read in a loud whisper from some worn novel out of the library at

Anna Bronstein

David Bronstein

L. D. Bronstein aged nine

film of life has no end, and I was only at the beginning... By the light of the blacksmith's forge or the kitchen fire, I often saw my parents, my relatives and our neighbours in quite a new way.'

In the autumn of 1888, at the age of nine, Lev Davidovich left the backwater of Yanovka for the busy Black Sea port of Odessa – 'commercial, multi-racial, loudly coloured'. There he lived with his mother's nephew, Moissei Filipovich Spentzer, a cultured liberal whose wife was a school-teacher and who himself later became a distinguished publisher. After some difficulty, due to the restrictions on Jews entering State secondary schools, the boy was admitted to St Paul's *Realschule*; this differed from the normal *Gymnasium* in that Latin and Greek were not taught there, and pupils received wider instruction in mathematics, science and modern languages. He at once reached the top of his class, and his intelligence made him popular with his masters – although at one point he was temporarily expelled for leading a revolt against a disliked teacher. At school he developed a passion for mathematics, while in the artistic and intellectual atmosphere of the Spentzer household he fell under the spell of literature: Tolstoy, Goethe, Dickens, Pushkin, Nekrassov. He started a school magazine; both the theatre and the world of journalism held a glamour for him.

'In 1894 Alexander III died. As usual on such occasions, the liberal hopes sought support from the heir to the throne. He replied with a kick. At the audience granted to the Zemstvo leaders, the young Tsar (Nicholas II) described their aspirations for a constitution as "nonsensical dreams" . . . I was fifteen at the time. I was unreservedly on the side of the nonsensical dreams, and not on that of the Tsar. Vaguely I believed in a gradual development which would bring backward Russia nearer to advanced Europe. Beyond that my political ideas did not go . . . In 1895 Friedrich Engels died. Secret reports were read at meetings held in his memory by student groups in the various cities of Russia. I was then in my sixteenth year. But I did not even know the name of Engels, and could hardly say anything definite about Marx.'

St Paul's had only six forms, instead of the usual seven, so in order to matriculate Lev Davidovich had to spend his final year at a similar school in the nearby provincial town of Nikolayev. He arrived there in the summer of 1896. This move, he later wrote, was the turning-point of his youth, 'for it raised within me the question of my place in human society'.

At Nikolayev Lev Davidovich lodged with a family whose sons were drawn to Socialism. For several months he scornfully dismissed their 'Socialist Utopias' – and then he suddenly declared himself a convert. As Isaac Deutscher writes in *The Prophet Armed*: 'Again and again we shall see this psychological mechanism at work in him: He is confronted with a new idea to which up to a point he is conditioned to respond; yet he resists at first with stubborn haughtiness; his resistance grows with the attraction; and he subdues incipient doubt and

Bobrinetz, following the words with her toil-stained finger. She often grew confused, and faltered over some especially long sentence. Sometimes an explanation from any one of the children would throw an entirely new light for her on the story she had been reading. But she continued to read perseveringly and untiringly, and on quiet winter days we could hear her monotonous whisper as far as the front hall . . .

'The reapers received forty to fifty roubles for the four summer months, and their board. The open field was their home in fine weather; in bad weather they took shelter under the haystacks . . . They never had any meat. Vegetable fat was all they ever got, and that in small quantities. This diet was sometimes a ground for complaint. The labourers would leave the fields and collect in the courtyard. They would lie face downward in the shade of the barn, brandishing their bare, cracked, straw-pricked feet in the air, and wait to see what would happen. Then my father would give them some water-melons, or half a sack of dried fish, and they would go back to work again, often singing . . .

'In the machine-shop, the kitchen and the backyard, a life stretched before me which was different from and more spacious than the one I led in my own family. The

hesitation. Then his inner defences crumble, his self-confidence begins to vanish; but he is still too proud or not convinced enough to give any sign of yielding . . . Then, suddenly, the new conviction hardens in him, and, as if in a single moment, overcomes his spirit of contradiction and vanity. He startles his erstwhile opponents not merely by his complete and disinterested surrender, but by the enthusiasm with which he embraces their cause, and sometimes by the unexpected and far-reaching conclusions which he draws from their arguments.'

His new friends introduced him to a poor gardener called Franz Shvigovsky, who rented an orchard on the outskirts of the town where a small group of radical students met regularly in a hut to discuss political ideas. Lev Davidovich joined this circle, which also included a number of old Narodniks living under police surveillance in the neighbourhood. Almost immediately, he embraced the romantic attitude to revolution of the Populists. But the group contained one solitary Marxist – perhaps its most interesting member. She is described by Max Eastman in *Leon Trotsky, The Portrait Of A Youth* (1926): 'Alexandra Lvovna Sokolovskaya was six years older than Trotsky, and had lived through some of the darkest years of the reaction which followed the failure of the terrorists

Nikolayev, 1897 – Alexandra Lvovna Sokolovskaya with her brother Ilya on her right, L. D. Bronstein on her left, and Dr G. A. Ziv, a fellow-conspirator, at her feet
Right: L. D. Bronstein aged eighteen

in Russia. Born in utter poverty and reared by a father who loved the ideal of liberty, she had herself long ago accepted the rebel mood and philosophy of the Narodniks.' Then she had read an account of the trial of Vera Zasulich – who, in 1878, had shot General Trepov, head of the St Petersburg police, in protest against the flogging of political prisoners. The trial exposed such hideous abuses by the police that she was acquitted. Alexandra, writes Eastman, 'could not endure the inaction, the pessimism, the dull colour of revolutionary faith among her contemporaries. She was the new generation – she resolved to go again among the people and teach revolt.'

During a course in midwifery at the University of Odessa, she met students who had worked in Geneva with Zasulich herself, sending illegal Marxist literature into Russia.

'She became a resolute adherent of this new and more coldly scientific method for the regeneration of her country and the world. She had read enough to know that the boys in Shvigovsky's garden were as ignorant as they were brilliant . . . She remembers how they first announced to her the arrival of Bronstein: "Here is the man who can talk to you! Such logic! *Nobody* can beat him!" Expecting some momentous and whiskered professor, who would "inform her of the errors underlying the economic system of Karl Marx", she was utterly amazed when this smooth young child appeared with the close-cropped black hair and the pale-blue eyes. Was this the great anti-Marxist debater they had been telling her about? But he was! From the first crackle of that voice she felt the attack, and she defended herself sharply, ironically. Not only on that occasion, but every time thereafter when they met, some sarcastic tilt would take place. "You still think you're a Marxist? I can't imagine how a young girl so full of life can stand that dry, narrow, impractical stuff!" "I can't imagine how a person who thinks he is logical can be contented with a headful of vague, idealistic emotions!"'

This apparently antagonistic relationship, which thrived on insulting repartee, really concealed a mutual attraction. Lev Davidovich collaborated with Alexandra's brother Ilya on an anti-Marxist play: to their surprise, they found that the Populist hero emerged as a feeble character, 'while all the courage, youth and hope were with the young Marxists . . .' The 'psychological mechanism' began to work again in Lev Davidovich, who now paid closer attention to the inadequate supply of Marxist literature available to him. He noticed that the industrial development of Russia was spreading

south-east to the Ukraine; about ten thousand workers were employed at Nikolayev in the docks and in two big factories. In the spring of 1897, according to Dr G. A. Ziv, a medical student from Kiev who attended Shvigovsky's meetings, 'Bronstein suddenly called me aside and proposed in great secrecy that I join a working-men's association, organized by himself. The Narodnik idea, Bronstein said, had been discarded; the association was planned to be social democratic...'

The Southern Russian Workers' Union, as this organization was called, circulated leaflets and a broadsheet, *Our Cause*, among the dockers and factory-hands. 'What satisfaction I had when I received the information from factories and work-shops that the workers avidly read the mysterious leaflets printed in purple ink,' Trotsky wrote later. 'They imagined the author as a strange and powerful person who had . . . penetrated into all the factories, and within twenty-four hours reacted to events with fresh leaflets.' The success of this clandestine activity did not prevent him from graduating with honours in the summer of 1897. The police, unable to believe that the agitation in the factories and docks could be traced to the handful of adolescent cranks who met in Shvigovsky's hut, did not round up the conspirators until January 1898. Two hundred people were arrested – including the six intellectuals at the head of the movement, who had previously agreed not to hide in the event of discovery. Lev Davidovich spent three weeks in an icy cell at Nikolayev, followed by two and a half months of solitary confinement in the Kherson gaol. In May he was transferred to a prison at Odessa, where one of the warders happened to bear the name of Trotsky. Here he read Darwin and wrote a materialistic history of freemasonry: his long resistance to Marxism had finally collapsed.

During the autumn of 1899 he was moved to the Butyrsky transfer-prison in Moscow and reunited with his colleagues from the orchard: Alexandra and her brothers, Shvigovsky, Ziv and other friends. They came up for trial early in 1900: the ring-leaders, including Lev Davidovich, were sentenced to four years' exile in Eastern Siberia. 'After this we were still kept for over six months in the Moscow transfer-prison. I used the interim for intensive studies in theory. Then for the first time I heard of Lenin, and studied his book on the development of Russian capitalism, which had just appeared, from cover to cover.' In the spring, he and Alexandra were married; neither believed in this formality, but it was necessary to ensure that their exile would be shared. The service was conducted by a Jewish chaplain in a cell, and the wedding-ring was borrowed from one of the prison guards. 'We were sent away from the Moscow prison in the summer. There were interludes in other prisons. It wasn't until the autumn of 1900 that we reached our place of banishment.'

They lived, with their baby daughter Zina, in a series of little towns above the Arctic Circle where life was 'dark and repressed, utterly remote from the world'. In Siberia he made his first serious study of *Das Kapital*,

L. D. Bronstein in Siberia

'brushing the cockroaches from the pages', and organized local union activity. He also contributed a vast quantity of articles – literary criticism and vivid atmospheric sketches – to a newspaper published at Irkutsk, the closest link with civilization. Perhaps the most eloquent statement of his feelings at this period is contained in an essay on *Optimism and Pessimism*, written early in 1901.

'If I were one of the celestial bodies, I would look with complete detachment upon this miserable ball of dust and dirt . . . I would shine upon the good and the evil alike . . . But I am a *man*. World history which to you, dispassionate gobbler of science, to you, book-keeper of eternity, seems only a negligible moment in the balance of time, is to me everything! As long as I breathe, I shall fight for the future, that radiant future in which man, strong and beautiful, will become master of the drifting stream of his history and will direct it towards the boundless horizon of beauty, joy and happiness! . . .

'It seems as if the new century, this gigantic newcomer, were bent at the very moment of its appearance on driving the optimist into absolute pessimism and civic nirvana. "Death to Utopia! Death to faith! Death to love! Death to hope!" thunders the twentieth century in salvoes of fire and in the rumbling of guns. "Surrender, you pathetic dreamer. Here I am, your long-awaited twentieth century, your 'future'."

'"No", replies the unhumbled optimist. "You – you are only the *present*."'

A second daughter, Nina, was born to the Bronsteins in 1902. That summer they received a copy of Lenin's book *What Is To Be Done?* and heard of 'a Marxist newspaper published abroad, the *Iskra*, which had as its object the creation of a centralised organisation of professional revolutionaries who would be bound together by the iron rule of action. My hand-written essays, newspaper articles and proclamations for the Siberian Union immediately looked small and provincial to me . . . I had to escape from exile . . . Life under conditions in Siberia was not easy, and my escape would place a double burden on the shoulders of Alexandra Lvovna. But she met this objection with the two words: "You must". Duty to the revolution overshadowed everything else for her, personal relations especially . . . Life separated us, but nothing could destroy our friendship and our intellectual kinship.'

Placing a dummy figure in his bed (which successfully deceived a police inspector the following evening), he left his family one summer night in 1902, hidden beneath a bundle of hay on a peasant's cart. His friends at Irkutsk provided him with a false passport: at random, he picked the name of his former gaoler to designate his new identity, and it was as Leon Trotsky that he boarded a train on the Trans-Siberian Railway. He left it at Samara, where the Russian branch of *Iskra* was situated. Here his literary reputation was already established, and he found that his articles had earned him the nickname of The Pen (*Piero*). Soon a message from Lenin reached Samara: The Pen was asked to report immediately to

Iskra's headquarters abroad. Trotsky's first foreign exile had begun.

Trotsky managed to get himself from Samara to Vienna, but when he arrived there he was penniless. He boldly disturbed the Sunday rest of Victor Adler, leader of the Austrian Social Democrats, who staked him as far as Zurich, where Paul Axelrod lived. Axelrod, with George Plekhanov and Vera Zasulich, represented the older generation among *Iskra*'s six editors: pioneers of social democracy in Russia, they had been émigrés since the 1880s. The other members of the editorial board – Vladimir Ilyich Lenin, Jules Martov and Alexander Potresov – were much younger (Lenin was thirty-two) and had only recently left Russia. All lived in London,

Alexandra in Siberia, with other political exiles

Alexandra (seated second from left), shortly after Trotsky's escape from Siberia. She is holding her baby daughter Nina, and Zina is held by the woman on the right

Vladimir Ilyich Lenin

Nadezhada Konstantinovna Krupskaya

with the exception of Plekhanov and Axelrod in Switzerland. Penniless again, Trotsky woke Axelrod in the middle of the night and was given enough money to travel to Paris and on to London. He arrived early one morning in October 1902, penniless once more but armed with a scrap of paper bearing a scribbled address: 30 Holford Square, King's Cross. This was the house where Lenin was living, in one room and a kitchen, with his wife Nadezhda Konstantinovna Krupskaya; they were known to their neighbours as Mr and Mrs Richter. Trotsky took a cab straight there and, following instructions, knocked loudly three times. The door was opened by Krupskaya, who called out to Lenin, still in bed, 'The Pen has arrived!' The welcoming expression on Lenin's face, Trotsky noticed, 'was tinged with a justifiable amazement'. After Krupskaya had paid the cabman and made some coffee, she returned to find 'Vladimir Ilyich still seated on the bed in animated conversation with Trotsky on some abstract theme'.

Krupskaya found Trotsky a room in a nearby house, where Martov and Zasulich were already installed.

'Either the same or the next morning', Trotsky recalled, 'Vladimir Ilyich and I went for a long walk around London. From a bridge, Lenin pointed out Westminster and some other famous buildings. I don't remember the exact words he used, but what he conveyed was: "This is their famous Westminster", and "their" referred of course not to the English but to the ruling classes . . . To his eyes, the invisible shadow of the ruling classes always overlay the whole of human culture – a shadow that was as real to him as daylight.'

Trotsky began to write for *Iskra*, and gave a public lecture in Whitechapel on 'What is Historic Materialism, and how do the Social-Revolutionaries understand it?' This was such a success ('I returned home, I remember, as if I were walking on air') that he was sent on a lecture tour of Brussels, Liége and Paris. A telegram summoned him from Paris to London: he was to be smuggled illegally back into Russia, where manpower was short after wholesale arrests of suspected revolutionaries. But the plan was altered; Leon Deutsch – a respected figure in émigré circles who had organized the Group for the Emancipation for Labour with Plekhanov, Zasulich and Axelrod in 1883 in order to propagate Marxism in Russia – persuaded Lenin that 'the youth' needed to live longer abroad to complete his political education. In March 1903, Lenin suggested that Trotsky should be appointed *Iskra*'s seventh editor, to preserve a balance between the two opposing groups of three. All his colleagues agreed, with the single important exception of Plekhanov, who firmly vetoed the proposal on the grounds that Trotsky's literary style was too floridly rhetorical. Plekhanov's taste was hard to please; he also criticized Lenin's articles for having no style at all.

Plekhanov and Axelrod, who had been close associates for over twenty years, were sharply contrasted characters. Axelrod had no gift for writing or for oratory; he earned his living as a worker, and passionately believed that the proletariat would come to socialism without leadership from the intelligentsia. Plekhanov was a brilliant speaker and a polished stylist, with an aristocratic manner and an intellectual approach to socialism. From the start he was bitterly jealous of Trotsky, whose precocious talents threatened to eclipse his own; while Trotsky was immediately drawn to the simple goodness of Axelrod, like himself a Jew from the Southern Ukraine.

In London and Geneva – where the *Iskra* offices were transferred in April 1903 – Trotsky saw much more of Zasulich and Martov than he did of Lenin. 'Vera Zasulich', he wrote, 'was an exceptional person; she was also charming in a peculiar manner. She wrote very slowly, truly suffering all the torments of creation. "Vera does not write", Vladimir Ilyich once said. "She composes a mosaic" . . . She was, and she remained to the end, the old type of Radical intellectual with Marxism grafted on to her by fate . . . The word "revolutionary" had for her a particular meaning devoid of any connotation of class consciousness . . . *Iskra* was under Lenin's political direction; the main contributor was, however, Martov. He wrote with ease, and interminably; just the way he talked . . . Lenin disliked those long palavers, formless debates and interminable chaotic conversations which inevitably led to émigré gossip and empty chatter. Martov, however, was inclined to this kind of pastime . . . [He] lived much more in the present, with day-to-day news, polemics and conversations. Lenin, although firmly entrenched in the present, was always trying to pierce the veil of the future. Martov evolved innumerable and often brilliant guesses, hypotheses and propositions, which he himself promptly forgot; whereas Lenin waited and developed his ideas when he needed them.'

Krupskaya worked as secretary to the editorial board. Trotsky describes her as at the very centre of the organization: 'She . . . received comrades when they arrived, instructed them when they left, established connections, supplied secret addresses, wrote letters, and coded and decoded correspondence. In her room there was always a smell of burned paper from the secret letters she heated over the fire to read. She often complained, in her gently insistent way, that people did not write enough, or that they got the code all mixed up, or

A copy of *Iskra* (The Spark). Top: 30 Holford Square

wrote in chemical ink in such a way that one line covered another, and so forth.' Trotsky's relationship with Lenin was to pass through many violent vicissitudes, but Krupskaya's early affection for 'the young eagle' remained constant. Years later, after Lenin's death in 1924, she wrote to tell Trotsky 'that about a month before his death, as he was looking through your book, Vladimir Ilyich stopped at the place where you sum up Marx and Lenin, and asked me to read it over again to him; he listened very attentively, and then looked it over again himself. And here is another thing I want to tell you. The attitude of V.I. towards you when you came to us in London from Siberia remained unchanged until his death . . .'

On his first visit to Paris in the autumn of 1902, Trotsky had met an attractive young woman called Natalya Ivanovna Sedova. Born in the Ukraine in 1882, she came from a family of impoverished Russian gentlefolk and had been orphaned in her eighth year; some of her relations were connected with the Narodniks. Expelled from a private school at Kharkov for leading a demonstration against compulsory religious observance, she had attended a university for women in Moscow before moving to Geneva to study botany. Here she met students who had come under the influence of Plekhanov, and at the age of nineteen (like Alexandra before her) she was helping them smuggle illegal Marxist literature into Russia. She then joined the group of political émigrés associated with *Iskra* in Paris: when Trotsky had arrived there from Siberia, she found him an attic room in the house where she lodged. Shortly after this, they became lovers: she remained his cherished and devoted companion for the rest of his life, and bore him two sons. This new attachment, which was to prove so lasting, had no ill effect on Trotsky's relationship with Alexandra: all three were on terms of loyal and respectful friendship until their deaths.

Natalya tried to share her passion for art with Trotsky by taking him to the Louvre, but at first made little headway. 'He expressed his general impression of Paris in this way: "Resembles Odessa, but Odessa is better",' she later remembered. 'This absurd conclusion can be explained by the fact that L.D. was utterly absorbed in political life, and could see something else only when it forced itself upon him. He reacted to it as if it were a bother, something unavoidable.' Trotsky himself explained that 'I was resisting art as I had resisted revolution earlier in life, and later, Marxism; as I resisted, for several years, Lenin and his methods.' In 1903, Natalya took Trotsky, Lenin and Martov to the Opéra-Comique to hear Charpentier's *Louise*. This cultural experiment was a failure. Lenin had bought a new pair of shoes, but as they were too tight for him he had passed them on to Trotsky. 'I decided to wear them on the outing to the opera. On the way there everything went smoothly. But in the opera I began to feel very uncomfortable . . . On our way back my suffering became intolerable, with Vladimir Ilyich cruelly amusing himself at my expense.'

The forty-three delegates to the Second Congress of

Trotsky after his escape from Siberia
Left: Natalya Sedova as a young woman in Paris

Leon Deutsch and Paul Axelrod. Top: Jules Martov

the All-Russian Social Democratic Labour Party (which was to all intents and purposes its first) congregated in a verminous warehouse at Brussels on 30 July 1903. After four of the delegates had been deported by the Belgian police, the meetings were transferred to London, for a month of bitter debate in a hall near the Tottenham Court Road. Various trends were represented, including *Iskra* (which was in the majority), the Jewish Socialist Bund, and the 'Economists'. The latter (so called because of their concentration on such 'bread-and-butter' matters as wage increases to the exclusion of theory) wanted to keep the movement within the bounds of non-political trade unionism; while the Bund, and other semi-autonomous Social Democratic groups, preferred a loose federation to a highly centralized party which would impose strict discipline from above. With Trotsky's vehement support, Lenin succeeded in carrying various motions which resulted in the dissolution of all independent organizations and their fusion into a single Party with the *Iskra* group in complete command.

This triumph, however, revealed a split in the *Iskra* faction itself. Lenin and Plekhanov insisted that the Party statutes should restrict membership to 'any person who accepts its programme, supports the Party with material means and *personally participates in* one of its organizations'. Martov wished to substitute for the final phrase the much vaguer *'personally and regularly co-operates under the guidance of* one of its organizations'. Lenin feared that this subtle adjustment would admit any liberal sympathizer to the Party without submitting him to its discipline or requiring from him any positive action. Martov obtained a majority vote for his motion; but his supporters included the Bund and the other lesser groups, who then left the Congress – and the Party – in disgust.

Lenin's next controversial proposal was to cut by half the editorial board of *Iskra*, leaving it under the control of Plekhanov, Martov and himself. This meant getting rid of Axelrod, Vera Zasulich and Potresov, all of whom had taken Martov's side over the statutes. Martov and Trotsky energetically opposed Lenin's

Rosa Luxemburg, the Polish Social Democrat whom Trotsky first met in 1904, photographed in that year with Victor Adler

Vera Zasulich as a young woman

George Plekhanov

motion, but it was none the less carried by a majority of two votes. Lenin's supporters thus came ironically to be known as Bolsheviks (men of the majority) while Martov's faction were called Mensheviks (men of the minority). The situation contained further ironies: Lenin and Martov, formerly intimate friends, now found themselves enemies; Plekhanov (later the implacable opponent of the Bolshevik revolution) was at this time Lenin's strongest ally, and Trotsky (who with Lenin was to bring this revolution to success) his most articulate antagonist.

'How did I come to be with the "softs" at the congress?' Trotsky asked in *My Life*. Hindsight helped him towards the answer: 'Revolutionary centralism is a harsh, imperative and exacting principle. It often takes the guise of absolute ruthlessness in its relation to individual members, to whole groups of former associates. It is not without significance that the words "irreconcilable" and "relentless" are among Lenin's favourites. It is only the most impassioned revolutionary striving for a definite end – a striving that is utterly free from anything base or personal – that can justify such a personal ruthlessness. In 1903, the whole point at issue was nothing more than Lenin's desire to get Axelrod and Zasulich off the editorial board. My attitude towards them was full of respect, and there was an element of personal affection as well. Lenin also thought highly of them for what they had done in the past. But he believed that they were becoming an impediment for the future . . . It was my indignation at his attitude that really led to my parting with him at the second congress. His behaviour seemed unpardonable to me, both horrible and out-

rageous. And yet, politically it was right and necessary, from the point of view of organisation.'

After the Congress, Trotsky and the other Mensheviks boycotted both the Central Committee and *Iskra*. This unnerved Plekhanov, who soon decided to invite Axelrod, Zasulich, Martov and Potresov back on the editorial board. Lenin resigned from *Iskra* and broke with Plekhanov: 'I am absolutely convinced that you will come to the conclusion that it is impossible to work with the Mensheviks,' he told him. But it was to Trotsky that this prophecy was to prove applicable. Violently opposing the tendency towards an alliance between socialism and middle-class liberalism, which was typified by the old-fashioned idealism of Vera Zasulich, Trotsky left *Iskra* in April 1904, and formally announced his resignation from the Mensheviks in the following September. Yet in August he had published a pamphlet, *Our Political Tasks*, dedicated to Axelrod, which consisted of a fierce, and even personally abusive attack on the 'Jacobinism' of Lenin: 'A proletariat capable of exercising its dictatorship over society will not tolerate any dictatorship over itself,' he wrote. Thus the end of 1904 found Trotsky passionately dedicated to the Marxist revolution, but in double opposition to both the 'softness' of the Mensheviks and the rigid centralism of Lenin and the Bolsheviks.

In February 1905, Trotsky called once more at Victor Adler's house in Vienna. There he shaved off his moustache and beard. Events at St Petersburg had decided him to return to Russia – and it was necessary to disguise himself from recognition by the police.

The prestige of the Russian autocracy had been impaired by disastrous defeats abroad in the war with Japan, and by labour unrest at home. After some employees at the Putilov engineering works had been ruthlessly dismissed, all the Putilov workers came out on strike; soon other St Petersburg factories were at a standstill. The discontented citizens rallied to the Russian Workers' Assembly – an organization set up by a priest called Father George Gapon with the approval of the Minister of the Interior and backed by funds from the Secret Police. Gapon and his supporters composed a naïve and emotional protest in the form of a petition to Nicholas II. On 22 January 1905, he led over twenty thousand workers in a march to the Winter Palace to present this innocent document; but the Tsar was away and Imperial troops opened fire on the crowd. The number of people killed and wounded is impossible to ascertain – estimates vary between four hundred and four thousand – but the psychological damage was immense. Shortly after 'Bloody Sunday' the Grand-Duke Sergei, Governor-General of Moscow, was assassinated; it was news of this event that reached Trotsky in Vienna and incited him to action.

Natalya went on ahead of him to Kiev, and he joined her there in February with a passport in the name of a retired corporal called Arbuzov. He then moved to St Petersburg, where he became well known in revolutionary circles as 'Petr Petrovich'. When Natalya was arrested at a May-day meeting, it was necessary for him to go into hiding, and he left for Finland. Here he was able finally to formulate his conception of the political future. To quote *My Life*: 'Russia, I wrote then, is facing a bourgeois-democratic revolution. The basis of the revolution is the land question. Power will be captured by the class or the party which will lead the peasantry against Tsarism and the landowners. Neither the liberals nor the democratic intelligentsia will be able to do so; their historical time has passed. The revolutionary foreground is already occupied by the proletariat. Only the Social Democracy, acting through workers, can make the peasantry follow its lead . . . But once in control, the proletariat party will not be able to confine itself merely to the democratic programme; it will be obliged to adopt Socialist measures. How far it will go in that direction will depend not only on the correlation of forces in Russia itself, but on the entire international situation as well.'

In June, the mutiny of the battleship *Potemkin* had led to a strike in Odessa. A printers' strike in Moscow got off to a lame start in October, but then suddenly spread to the railways and throughout the country. All over Russia, workers were demanding constitutional reforms as well as higher wages and shorter hours. The first Soviet (or Council) of Workers' Delegates was formed and met on 14 October at the Technological Institute; Trotsky returned to St Petersburg in time to address it the following day. Under the pseudonym of Yanovsky, he soon became the Soviet's Chairman and its leading spirit: he was now twenty-six years old. The Tsar, alarmed by the general strike, issued a Manifesto on 17 October promising a constitution, civil liberties and universal suffrage. Trotsky led a huge crowd from the Technological Institute to the University. 'Citizens!' he cried. 'Now that we have put our foot on the neck of the ruling clique, they promise us freedom . . . Our strength is in ourselves. With sword in hand we must defend freedom. The Tsar's Manifesto . . . see! it is only a scrap of paper.'

Father Gapon and the Governor-General of St Petersburg with members of the Russian Workers' Assembly in January 1905

Parvus, Trotsky and Leon Deutsch together in the House of Preliminary Detention at St Petersburg, 1906

He waved the Manifesto in front of the crowd and, with a theatrical gesture, crumpled it in his fist. 'Today it has been given us and tomorrow it will be taken away and torn into pieces as I am now tearing it into pieces, this paper-liberty, before your eyes.'

Natalya, who had been in prison since May, was now released and rejoined Trotsky in St Petersburg. Here, as Mr and Mrs Vikentiev, they lived throughout the fifty days that the Soviet lasted – a period dominated by the energetic personality of Trotsky himself. 'A revolutionary chaos is not at all like an earthquake or a flood,' he remembered later. 'In the confusion of a revolution, a new order begins to take shape instantly; men and ideas distribute themselves naturally in new channels. Revolution appears as utter madness only to those whom it sweeps aside and overthrows. To us it was different. We were in our own element, albeit a stormy one. A time and place was found for everything. Some were even able to lead personal lives, to fall in love, to make new friends and actually to visit revolutionary theatres.' On 2 December the Soviet published a financial manifesto in which it prophesied the inevitable bankruptcy of Tsarism and warned that the debts incurred by the Romanovs would not be recognized by the victorious nation. The people were called upon to stop paying taxes and to withdraw deposits from the banks. The next day, a mass arrest by the police rounded up all the members of the St Petersburg Soviet. Trotsky spent a short time in the Kresty prison and in solitary confinement at the Peter-Paul fortress before being moved to await trial at the House of Preliminary Detention. The 'dress-rehearsal' for the revolution was over.

In the House of Detention Trotsky was allowed to receive visits from his lawyer and to communicate with other detainees. These included two old friends: Leon Deutsch and Alexander Helphand, a Russian Jew who under the pen-name of 'Parvus' had become celebrated in Germany as a scholarly Marxist economist. Trotsky had stayed with Parvus at Munich in the autumn of 1904, and during the days of the Soviet they had together edited the *Russian Gazette*, which they transformed from a paper with a tiny circulation into a fighting organ for the

Trotsky in his cell before the trial of the Soviet

masses. Parvus had also written the fatal 'financial manifesto'.

Trotsky describes him as 'unquestionably one of the most important of the Marxists at the turn of the century', but adds that there was always something mad and unreliable about him. 'In addition to all his other ambitions, this revolutionary was torn by an amazing desire to get rich . . . In spite of his originality and ingenuity of thought, he failed utterly as a leader.' Deutsch wanted to plan a mass escape from prison, and easily persuaded Parvus to agree; but Trotsky opposed the suggestion. 'I was attracted by the political importance

Defendants and their lawyers at the trial of the Soviet: Trotsky is standing in the centre, holding papers

of the trial ahead.'

The trial of the Soviet of Workers' Delegates opened on 19 September 1906. The case was heard in an atmosphere of relative freedom; over two hundred witnesses gave evidence, revealing under cross-examination many examples of violence and corruption on the part of the government and the police. Trotsky's parents were in the audience; they seem to have been confusedly impressed by their son's celebrity, which partially blinded them to the seriousness of his situation. 'My mother was sure that I would not only be acquitted, but even given some mark of distinction . . . My father was pale, silent, happy and distressed, all in one.' On 4 October Trotsky made a long speech, in which he concentrated on the main charge, that of insurrection. 'A popular insurrection cannot be staged. It can only be foreseen.' The Soviet, he claimed, had tried to organize and educate the masses; it was not preparing an insurrection so much as preparing itself for one. The

masses had no arms; the victory of a popular rising would be brought about less by their ability to kill others than by 'their great readiness to die themselves'. He would admit that the Soviet, in this sense, had armed the workers for a direct struggle against the 'existing form of government', but questioned whether any form of government had really existed at all. 'What we possess is not a national governmental force but a machine for mass murder.'

A government official was prepared to testify that the police had been planning a bloody pogrom which the formation of the Soviet had averted; when the court refused to call him to the witness stand, the defendants broke up the trial by insisting on returning to their cells. The defence counsel, the witnesses and the public then walked out as well; and on 2 November the judges delivered their verdict to a court-room empty of everyone except the prosecuting lawyer. The members of the Soviet were found not guilty of insurrection; but Trotsky and fourteen others were sentenced to loss of civic rights and 'enforced settlement' in Siberia. This was a harsher

Convicted members of the Soviet on the journey to Obdorsk: Trotsky second from left. Fifty-five soldiers and policemen guarded the

handful of prisoners. 'Every day', Trotsky wrote to Natalya, 'we descend one degree farther into the kingdom of cold and barbarism'

punishment than the 'administrative exile' to which he had been condemned in 1900; it meant deportation for life, and any attempt at escape carried an additional penalty of three years' hard labour. On 5 January 1907, the convicts, dressed in grey prison uniforms, set off on their slow and dismal journey. They were bound for the penal colony at Obdorsk, on the Polar circle, a thousand miles from the nearest railway station.

Always a fluent and prolific author, Trotsky had taken advantage of the long days in prison before the trial to enlarge his literary output. Of his numerous writings during 1906, the most important was *Results and Prospects*, which he conceived as a long concluding chapter to his collection of essays and chronicles on the events of 1905. It contained the first formulation of his theory of the Permanent Revolution, described by Isaac Deutscher as 'the most radical restatement, if not revision, of the prognosis of Socialist revolution undertaken since Marx's *Communist Manifesto*'. This theory, later regarded as the quintessence of Trotskyism, was to be the subject of bitter, and even murderous controversy in the future. Its basic content was summarized in 1929 by Trotsky himself in his Introduction to a later work, *The Permanent Revolution:*

'The theory of the permanent revolution, which originated in 1905 . . . pointed out that the democratic tasks of the backward bourgeois nations led directly, in our epoch, to the dictatorship of the proletariat and that the dictatorship of the proletariat puts socialist tasks on the order of the day. Therein lay the central idea of the theory. While the traditional view was that the road to the dictatorship of the proletariat led through a long period of democracy, the theory of the permanent revolution established the fact that for backward countries the road to democracy passed through the dictatorship of the proletariat. Thus democracy is not a regime that remains self-sufficient for decades, but is only a direct prelude to the socialist revolution. Each is bound to the other by an unbroken chain. Thus there is established between the democratic revolution and the socialist reconstruction of society a permanent state of revolutionary development.

'The second aspect of the theory has to do with the socialist revolution as such. For an indefinitely long time and in constant internal struggle, all social relations undergo transformation. Society keeps on changing its skin. Each stage of transformation stems directly from the preceding. This process necessarily retains a political character, that is, it develops through collisions between various groups in the society, which is in transformation. Outbreaks of civil war and foreign wars alternate with periods of "peaceful" reform. Revolutions in economy, technique, science, the family, morals, and everyday life develop in complex reciprocal action and do not allow society to achieve equilibrium. Therein lies the permanent character of the socialist revolution as such.

'The international character of the socialist revolution, which constitutes the third aspect of the theory of the permanent revolution, flows from the present state of the economy and the social structure of humanity. Internationalism is no abstract principle but a theoretical and political reflection of the character of world economy, of the world development of productive forces, and of the world scale of the class struggle. The socialist revolution begins on national foundations – but cannot be completed on these foundations alone. The maintenance of the proletarian revolution within a national framework can only be a provisional state of affairs . . . In an isolated proletarian dictatorship, the internal and external contradictions grow inevitably along with the successes achieved. If it remains isolated, the proletarian state must finally fall victim to these contradictions. The way out for it lies only in the victory of the proletariat of the advanced countries. Viewed from this standpoint, a national revolution is not a self-contained whole; it is only a link in the

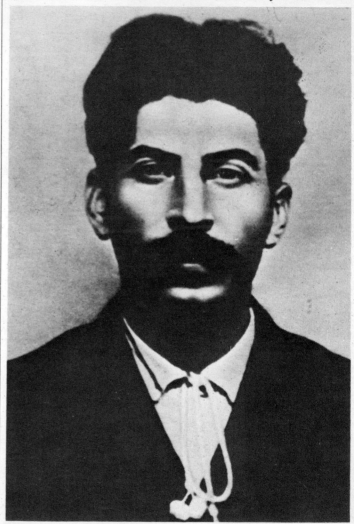

The young Joseph Stalin

international chain. The international revolution constitutes a permanent process, despite temporary declines and ebbs.'

After travelling for thirty-three days, Trotsky and the convict party stopped at a place called Beresov, about 330 miles short of Obdorsk. He pretended to be suffering from sciatica, and was allowed to stay behind in a hospital. Supervision was minimal, as it was considered impossible for anyone to get away through the uncharted wastes and the February blizzards. None the less, Trotsky succeeded in effecting his second Siberian escape, driven by deer in a sleigh over the endless snow. He covered 430 miles in a week before reaching the Urals, where he posed as an engineer and continued his journey by horse until he could board a train. Natalya was living in Finland alone with her baby son, Lyova, who had been born while his father was in prison. She was amazed to receive a cable from Trotsky asking her to meet him at the 'railway junction'; unfortunately, the telegraphist had omitted the name of the station. She hurried to St Petersburg, where she got on a train going in what she hoped was the right direction. It stopped at a junction called Samino at the same time as another train coming from the Urals. 'I ran out of the station,' she remembered. 'Nobody there. I jumped into the other train, ran through one car after another, and he was not there. Suddenly I recognized L.D.'s fur coat in a compartment . . . I leaped out of the car, and immediately ran into L.D. who was rushing out of the station looking

Natalya Sedova in Vienna

for me.' He had completed the entire journey in eleven days, and the news of his escape had not yet reached St Petersburg.

Trotsky returned with Natalya to Finland, where both Martov and Lenin were living. Martov, Trotsky noted, had many brilliant and subtle ideas, but not the most important of all: 'He did not know what to do next . . . Lenin spoke approvingly of my work in prison, but he taunted me for not drawing the necessary conclusions, in other words, for not going over to the Bolsheviks.' Trotsky remained near Helsingfors with Natalya and little Lyova for a while, and then embarked on a steamer bound for Sweden and his second foreign exile.

By the end of April 1907, he was back in London for another Party Congress, the fifth and last, held at the Brotherhood Church in Whitechapel. Here Trotsky met Maxim Gorki for the first time, and renewed acquaintanceship with Rosa Luxemburg, whom he had known slightly for three years. He described her as 'a little woman, frail, and even sickly looking, but with a noble face, and beautiful eyes that radiated intelligence; she captivated one by the sheer courage of her mind and character . . . On the question of the so-called permanent revolution, Rosa took the same stand as I did. In this connection, Lenin and I once had a half-humorous conversation in the lobby. The delegates stood about us in a close ring. "It is all because she does not speak Russian too well", he said. To which I retorted: "But she speaks excellent Marxian."'

It is possible that the ring of delegates may have included a rather mysterious visitor from Tiflis called Koba, whose real name was Joseph Djugashvili and who was later to be known as Stalin. He claimed to represent the Bolshevik workers in the Borchalo district, although no local party branch existed there. On his return to Russia, Koba wrote a description of the Congress in which he attacked the internationalism of the Mensheviks. 'Somebody among the Bolsheviks remarked jestingly that since the Mensheviks were the faction of the Jews and the Bolsheviks that of native Russians, it would become us to make a pogrom in the party.' The Congress had been sharply divided between the two factions; Trotsky still belonged to neither, and Koba, quoting Lenin, described Trotsky's contribution to the debates as 'beautifully useless'. Koba had himself kept silent at the meetings, and Trotsky did not even notice his presence there.

By the end of 1907, Trotsky had settled with Natalya and Lyova in Vienna, where their second son Sergei was born. At first, they occupied an attractive villa, but a rise in rent soon forced them to move into three bare rooms in a working-class suburb. This was to be Trotsky's base for seven years – 'the years of reaction'. He would have preferred to live in Berlin, where Rosa Luxemburg and Karl Liebknecht led the radical wing of the German Social Democratic Party, but the vigilance of the police there made this impossible. Political life in Austria, which centred round Victor Adler, depressed Trotsky and reminded him of the antics of a squirrel in a cage. His parents came to Europe in 1910, bringing with them his elder daughter, Zina; not long after their return to Russia, he heard that his mother had died at Yanovka. Trotsky described his work during this long fallow period as 'consisting chiefly of interpreting the revolution of 1905, and of paving the way for the next revolution by theoretical research'. He wrote regularly in a democratic Russian paper, *Kievan Thought*, for which he covered the Balkan War in 1912. Since 1908 he had also been editing *Pravda*, where he preached unity of the party and bitterly attacked the Bolsheviks; he was understandably furious when, in 1912, Lenin's faction began to publish a daily in St Petersburg with the same name. Trotsky had no idea that the rival paper had been set up by a hitherto obscure Bolshevik, Joseph Djugashvili. However, an odd encounter took place in Vienna early in 1913, when Trotsky called on Skobolev, a young Menshevik who worked as his assistant on the Viennese *Pravda*. Isaac Deutscher gives a vivid account of it in *The Prophet Armed*:

'They were sitting by a *samovar* and talking when suddenly, without knocking at the door, there entered from another room a man of middle height, haggard, with a swarthy greyish face, showing marks of small-pox. The stranger, as if surprised by Trotsky's presence, stopped a moment at the door and gave a guttural growl, which might have been taken for a greeting. Then, with an empty glass in his hand, he went to the *samovar*, filled the glass with tea, and went out without saying a word. Skobolev explained that this was a Caucasian, Djugashvili, who had just become a member of the Bolshevik Central Committee and seemed to be acquiring some importance

Trotsky with his daughter Nina in France
Right: Trotsky's passport to Switzerland in order to attend the Zimmerwald conference in 1915

in it. Trotsky . . . noticed the Caucasian's "dim but not commonplace" appearance, "a morose concentration" in his face, and an expression of set hostility in his "yellow" eyes.'

On the outbreak of the First World War, all Russian émigrés – whether Bolsheviks, Mensheviks or Social Revolutionaries – were at first equally appalled to find the leaders of European socialism exhorting the working classes to fight and die in defence of the old régime. To avoid internment in Vienna, Trotsky and his family moved to Zurich in August 1914, where he wrote *The War and the International* – the first extensive condemnation of the war by a Russian socialist. In November he crossed the frontier into France as war correspondent for *Kievan Thought*; Natalya and his sons followed him six months later. In Paris, Martov was editing a journal called *The*

Voice, which later changed its name to *Our Word*; Trotsky became first a contributor and then co-editor. Through Pierre Monatte, editor of the syndicalist publication *La Vie Ouvrière*, he got to know Alfred Rosmer and started a friendship which was to last till Trotsky's death. Rosmer was at that time an anarcho-syndicalist journalist, but he was already tending towards Marxism and later became a founder of the French Communist Party. Trotsky's relationship with Martov, unfortunately, was to prove less enduring. 'Martov's first reaction to events was nearly always revolutionary, but before he could put his ideas on paper, his mind would be besieged by doubts . . . At the beginning of the war, he complained to Axelrod that events had driven him to the verge of insanity . . . When I arrived in Paris, I found him already fading.'

On 5 September 1915, thirty-eight delegates from eleven countries met at the small Swiss village of Zimmerwald for the first international socialist conference to debate the implications of the war. Most of the delegates were pacifists, but a minority, led by Lenin, urged the conference to transcend the pacifist position by adopting an attitude of revolutionary defeatism towards all belligerent governments and thus turn a squalid Imperialist war into a world-wide conflict between the classes. For the first time, Lenin was expressing an international, as opposed to an exclusively Russian, view of socialism, which was near to Trotsky's own conception of the permanent revolution. Trotsky, however, did not go as far as Lenin in calling for a civil war; he believed that the cause of socialism could only be furthered if the war ended 'with neither victors nor vanquished'. He was asked to draw up a statement of principles, and the eloquent result, which later became famous as the Zimmerwald Manifesto, was enthusiastically and unanimously adopted by the conference – although Lenin's group placed its reservations on record.

'Workers of Europe! The war has lasted for more than a year. Millions of corpses lie on the battlefields; millions of men have been crippled for life. Europe has become a gigantic human slaughterhouse . . . As the war proceeds, its real driving forces become apparent in all their baseness. Piece by piece the veil which has hidden the meaning of this world catastrophe from the understanding of the peoples is falling down. In every country the capitalists who forge the gold of war profits from the blood of the people are declaring that the war is for national defence, democracy, and the liberation of oppressed nationalities. THEY LIE! In reality they are burying on the fields of devastation the liberties of their own peoples, together with the independence of other nations. New fetters, new chains, new burdens are being brought into existence, and the workers of all countries, of the victorious as well as of the vanquished, will have to bear them . . .

'But the Socialist parties . . . have invited the workers to suspend the working-class struggle, the only possible and effective means of working-class emancipation. They have voted the ruling classes the credits for carrying on the war . . . They have given to their govern-

Signature du Titulaire :

Léon Trotsky

ments Socialist ministers as hostages for the observance of the national truce, and thus have taken on themselves the responsibility for this war, its aims, its methods . . . Organised Workers! Since the outbreak of the war you have put your energies, your courage, your steadfastness at the service of the ruling classes. Now the task is to enter the lists for your own cause, for the sacred aims of Socialism, for the salvation of the oppressed nations and the enslaved classes, by means of the irreconcilable working-class struggle . . .'

But after Zimmerwald, one by one, Trotsky's former friends disillusioned him by 'deserting the cause' and coming out in support of the war. Parvus (who was engaged in the Balkans on commercial enterprises to his

The unknown actor, appearing as a station-master with Clara Kimball Young in a scene from the Vitagraph film *My Official Wife*, whose slight resemblance to Trotsky started a false but persistent rumour that he had worked as a film extra at the Brooklyn studios
Top: the *Novy Mir* offices at 177 St Mark's Place, Lower East Side, New York

The order expelling Trotsky from France, signed by Louis Malvy, Minister of the Interior

own profit as well as the German Government's) announced his solidarity with the official line of the German Socialist leaders instead of that of Rosa Luxemburg and Karl Liebknecht. In Russia, Vera Zasulich and Potresov followed Plekhanov in the same direction. Trotsky, who had defended Zasulich against Lenin, felt betrayed. When his editorials in *Our Thought* began to preach co-operation with the Bolsheviks, Martov protested and after long-drawn-out arguments resigned from the paper, leaving Trotsky its sole editor.

This responsibility had inconvenient results: on 15 September 1916, the French police banned publication of *Our Thought*, and the following day Trotsky himself was ordered to leave the country. Pressure had clearly been brought to bear on Louis Malvy, the Minister of the

Interior, by the Embassy of Imperial Russia. Afraid that he would be extradited to Russia, Trotsky spent six fruitless weeks trying to get visas for Switzerland, Italy or Scandinavia; on 30 October he was arrested by the French police and deported to the Spanish frontier. At Madrid he 'viewed the treasures' in the Prado 'with the eagerness of a starved man'. An entry in his diary on this occasion shows that his appreciation of art had considerably matured since his first visit to the Louvre. 'Between us and these old artists – without in the least obscuring them or lessening their importance – there grew up before the war a new art, more intimate, more individualistic, one with greater nuances, at once more subjective and more intense. The war, by its mass passions and suffering, will probably wash away this mood and this manner for a long time – but that can never mean a simple return to the old form, however beautiful – to the anatomic and botanic perfection, to the Rubens thighs (though thighs are apt to play a great role in the new post-war art, which will be so eager for life).'

The Madrid police had received a telegram from the Paris *Préfecture* warning them of the presence of 'a dangerous anarchist' in their midst; Trotsky was arrested on 9 November and after three days in a Madrid prison was escorted to Cadiz. Here, loudly protesting, he was kept under police surveillance for six weeks. On 20 December he was taken to Barcelona, where he was joined by Natalya and the boys. The police bundled the family aboard a rickety little Spanish steamer, the *Monserrat*, which was sailing to the U.S.A. The other passengers struck him as 'deserters, adventurers, speculators, or simply "undesirables" thrown out of Europe'. His diary entry for Sunday, 13 January 1917, reads: 'We are nearing New York. At three o'clock in the morning, everybody wakes up. We have stopped. It is dark. Cold. Wind. Rain. On land, a wet mountain of buildings. The New World!'

Trotsky found lodgings in the Bronx for eighteen dollars a month, on East 164th Street and Stebbins Avenue. Modest enough by American standards, they contained an unexpected luxury: his first telephone. He immediately joined the editorial board of *Novy Mir* (*New World*), a paper published by Russian émigrés and edited by Nikolai Bukharin and Alexandra Kollontai. Many wild rumours were later current about the odd jobs he took in New York; but the unexciting truth is that he earned his living there exclusively by lecturing and journalism. In March, news reached America of disturbances in Petrograd: Sergei, ill with diphtheria at the time, jumped out of bed and executed a dance in celebration of the revolution. On 13 March, two days before the abdication of Nicholas II, Trotsky was writing in *Novy Mir*: 'We are the witnesses of the beginning of the second Russian revolution. Let us hope that many of us will be its participants.'

On 27 March, the jubilant family sailed out of New York harbour on a Norwegian freighter; but, to their bitter fury and disappointment, they were put out at Halifax, Nova Scotia, after only a week. British police, under orders from the Admiralty in London, arrested Trotsky and interned him in a prisoner-of-war camp at Amherst. The unpleasant conditions here left him with a life-long loathing of the British Government. There were over 800 Germans imprisoned at Amherst: Trotsky – Prisoner-of-War Number 1098 – told them of the Zimmerwald conference and the fight being waged by Karl Liebknecht against the Kaiser's war. He was amused when the prison officials interrupted this activity, confirming his view that Britain and Germany, apparently enemies, were allies in the face of anti-war subversion.

Released on 29 April, and tormented by impatience, he boarded a Danish vessel and with his family started on the maddeningly long sea voyage to Europe. At last they reached Finland, and Trotsky took a train to Petrograd, arriving there on 17 May (4 May in the old Russian calendar), exactly one month after Lenin. A delegation of internationalists had met him at the Russian frontier; at the capital a crowd, waving red banners, carried him shoulder-high from the station. His hour had come at last.

The prisoner-of-war form relating to Trotsky at Amherst Camp, Nova Scotia. Overleaf: Trotsky's triumphant return to Russia

Trotsky arrives at Petrograd station on 4 May, 1917

Power 1917-1921

Lenin and Trotsky in 1920

Trotsky (seventh from the left, second row) with members of the Soviet of Workers' and Soldiers' Deputies in 1917

Trotsky and Natalya, who had been away from Petrograd for ten years, were almost as bewildered as their two little boy Lyova and Sergei, at hearing Russian spoken in the streets and seeing Russian signs on the shops. They also had difficul in finding somewhere to live, but eventually secured one room for the whole family in the Kiev Hostelry. 'I think that went from the station straight to the meeting of the Executive Committee of the Soviet', Trotsky wrote in *My Life*. Tl

Chairman greeted him dryly. 'The Bolsheviks moved that I be elected to the Executive Committee, on the strength of my having been Chairman of the Soviet in 1905. This threw the committee into confusion. The Mensheviks and the Populists began whispering to one another. They had then an overwhelming majority in all the revolutionary institutions. Finally it was decided to include me in an advisory capacity. I was given my membership card and my glass of tea with black bread.'

The Mensheviks and the Populists (or Social Revolutionaries) had good reason for their uneasiness at Trotsky's reappearance: once their friend, he was now their opponent. The February revolution, which was ten weeks old when Trotsky returned to Russia, had so far led to little more than a succession of compromises with the ruling class. The Duma – a semi-parliamentary institution which had been set up after the 1905 revolution – had been dissolved, but the Temporary Committee of the Duma which had taken its place had included all the parties represented in the old Duma except for the extreme right wing and the Bolsheviks, whose deputies were in exile. At the same time, a new Soviet of Workers' and Soldiers' Deputies had come into being – a reincarnation of the 1905 Soviet. On the abdication of the Tsar, a Provisional Government had been formed, which consisted of the Temporary Committee supported by the Soviet. The leading figure in the Provisional Government was a Social Revolutionary, Alexander Kerensky, who was successively Minister of Justice, Minister of War, Prime Minister, Commander-in-Chief of the Army and President, during the eight muddled months in which this unsatisfactory and tentative 'dual power' was to govern Russia. Shortly before Trotsky's arrival, the Mensheviks and the Social Revolutionaries, who dominated the Soviet ('having passed through all the stages of vacillation known to nature', as Trotsky remarked), had decided that its 'support' of the Provisional Government should give way to a 'functional coalition'. On 5 May, Trotsky addressed the Soviet at the Smolny Institute: 'I consider this participation in the Ministry to be dangerous . . . The coalition government will not save us from the existing dualism of power; it will merely transfer that dualism into the Ministry itself.' The Soviet, however, voted in favour of the coalition, with only the Bolsheviks and a small group of Menshevik-Internationalists in opposition.

Trotsky and Lenin met, for the first time since Zimmerwald, on 7 May. It was an enlightening occasion for them both. Lenin learnt that Trotsky no longer believed in unity between Bolsheviks and Mensheviks, and was now in complete sympathy with the aims of the Bolshevik party; while Trotsky learnt that Lenin no longer believed that the outcome of the Russian revolution would be a 'democratic dictatorship of the proletariat and the peasantry' rather than a dictatorship of the proletariat itself. Indeed, Trotsky's own brother-in-law, Leo Borisovich Kamenev, a right-wing Bolshevik, had reproached Lenin with abandoning Bolshevism for Trotskyism and adopting wholesale the theory of the permanent revolution. The paths of Lenin and Trotsky, so long divergent, had been brought together by the war. The Mensheviks' betrayal of Zimmerwald had finally convinced Trotsky that the split in the socialist movement could never be healed; and the war had drawn Lenin's attention to the likelihood of revolution in the advanced European countries. Placing the Russian revolution in an international perspective, Lenin now acknowledged that the 'bourgeois' objectives of revolution in a backward country no longer applied to Russia.

Although the Bolshevik party was in a minority in the Soviet, its real power became apparent on 18 June, two days after Kerensky had launched an unpopular military offensive. The Soviet Congress, having banned a Bolshevik street demonstration, authorized another which was intended to show public confidence in the Soviet as a whole. The plan backfired, and the demonstration turned out to be spontaneously and overwhelmingly pro-Bolshevik. Isaac Babel's story *Line and Colour* describes Kerensky at this period failing to hold his audience: 'But after him Trotsky climbed to the speaker's tribune, twisted his mouth, and in an implacable voice began: "Comrades!"' Early in July, Petrograd was the scene of an unorganized uprising consisting of factory workers and soldiers, supplemented by 20,000 armed sailors from the revolutionary hotbed of Kronstadt. Trotsky's daughters, Zina and Nina, were shaken up by the unruly mob: 'One of them lost her glasses,' he wrote, 'both lost their hats, and both were afraid that they would lose the father who had just reappeared on their horizon.' Lacking leadership, the outbreak soon fizzled out: the Bolsheviks, who in fact considered it premature and had been unable to control it, were none the less accused of having inspired it. On 6 June, Kerensky's offensive ignominiously collapsed when the German army routed the Russian troops on the southern front. The Provisional Government, hoping to stabilize its position by persecution of the Bolsheviks, published documents which purported to prove that Lenin was a German spy: writs were issued against Lenin and five other Bolsheviks, including Alexandra Kollantai and two of his closest associates, Kamenev and Gregory Yevseyevich Zinoviev. Lenin and Zinoviev went into hiding in Finland, and Trotsky published a letter in which he proclaimed his solidarity with Lenin, although he was not yet officially a member of the Bolshevik party. The Ministry of Justice hesitated for two weeks before taking up the challenge; then on 23 July his arrest was ordered, and Trotsky found himself back again in the Kresty prison.

In August, a right-wing counter-revolution against the Provisional Government was led by General Kornilov, the Commander-in-Chief of the Army. A delegation from the sailors of Kronstadt visited Trotsky in prison to ask him whether they should defend Kerensky against Kornilov, or try to get rid of them both at the same time. He advised them to concentrate on Kornilov, as Kerensky's downfall was inevitable in the near future. The workers, organized by the Bolsheviks, sabotaged Kornilov's advance, which collapsed when his troops deserted. Trotsky was released on bail on 4 September: during his confinement, he had been elected to the Central Committee of the Bolshevik party, which by this time had a majority in the Soviets of Petrograd, Moscow and other industrial cities. On 23 September, by now an open Bolshevik, he became President of the Petrograd Soviet. Lenin, still in hiding, was urging the necessity for an immediate seizure of power by the Bolsheviks. In this he was supported by Trotsky, but vehemently opposed by Zinoviev and Kamenev. On 9 October – with the country in economic

Photo-montage of the Bolshevik leaders of the revolution

chaos – a Military Revolutionary Committee, headed by Trotsky, was formed at a session of the Soviet Executive; and on the following day the Bolshevik Central Committee, in Lenin's presence, adopted Lenin's resolution in favour of an armed insurrection by ten votes to two. Lenin went back into hiding for another two weeks; Zinoviev and Kamenev resumed their campaign against the uprising; and Trotsky set about mustering the forces of the revolution. N. Sukhanov has described Trotsky at this time: '. . . it seemed that he spoke everywhere simultaneously. Every worker and soldier of Petrograd knew him and listened to him. His influence on the masses and leaders alike was overwhelming. He was the central figure of those days, and the chief hero of this remarkable chapter of history.'

The insurrection of the Soviet forces, led by the Bolsheviks, began at two o'clock in the morning of 25 October. Trotsky, who had hardly moved out of the Smolny Institute for a week, addressed the Soviet eleven hours later. 'On behalf of the Military Revolutionary Committee, I declare that the Provisional Government is no longer existent . . . Railway stations, the post office, the telegraph, the Petrograd Telegraph Agency, the State Bank, have been occupied.'

Operations against the Winter Palace – the seat of the Provisional Government – began at nine o'clock that evening. Two hours later, the Second All-Russian Congress of the Soviets opened at the Smolny. Trotsky describes his experience of 'the deciding night' of 25 October in *My Life*: '. . . that evening, as we were waiting for the opening of the congress of the Soviets, Lenin and I were resting in a room adjoining the meeting-hall, a room entirely empty except for chairs. Someone had spread a blanket on the floor for us; someone else, I think it was Lenin's sister, had brought us pillows. We were lying side by side; body and soul were relaxing like overtaut strings. It was a well-earned rest. We could not sleep, so we talked in low voices. Only now did Lenin become reconciled to the postponement of the uprising. His fears had been dispelled. There was a rare sincerity in his voice. He was interested in knowing all about the mixed pickets of the Red Guards, sailors, and soldiers that had been stationed everywhere. "What a wonderful sight: a worker with a rifle, side by side with a soldier, standing before a street fire!" he repeated with deep feeling. At last the soldier and the worker had been brought together!

'Then he started suddenly. "And what about the Winter Palace?" I got up to ask, on the telephone, about the progress of the operations there, but he tried to stop me. "Lie still, I will send someone to find out." But we could not rest for long. The session of the congress of the Soviets was opening in the next hall. Ulyanova, Lenin's sister, came running to get me. "Dan is speaking. They are asking for you."'

Theodore Ilyich Dan was a Menshevik who had played a central part in the Provisional Government. Trotsky continues: 'In a voice that was breaking repeatedly, Dan was railing at the conspirators and

Trotsky (centre, in profile) greeted by German officers on his arrival at Brest Litovsk on 27 December, 1917

prophesying the inevitable collapse of the uprising. He demanded that we form a coalition with the Social-Revolutionists and the Mensheviks. The parties that had been in power only the day before, that had hounded us and thrown us into prison, now that we had overthrown them were demanding that we come to an agreement with them.

'I replied to Dan and, in him, to the yesterday of the revolution: "What has taken place is an uprising, not a conspiracy. An uprising of the masses of the people needs no justification. We have been strengthening the revolutionary energy of the workers and soldiers. We have been forging, openly, the will of the masses for an uprising. Our uprising has won. And now we are being asked to give up our victory, to come to an agreement.

With whom? You are wretched, disunited individuals; you are bankrupts; your part is over. Go to the place where you belong from now on – the dustbin of history!"'

Early the following morning, the Winter Palace fell to the insurgents and the Provisional Government was arrested. 'The power is taken over, at least in Petrograd. Lenin has not yet had time to change his collar, but his eyes are very wide awake, even though his face looks tired. He looks softly at me, with that sort of awkward shyness that with him indicates intimacy. "You know", he says hesitatingly, "from persecution and a life underground, to come so suddenly into power..." He pauses for the right word. "*Es schwindelt*", he concludes, changing suddenly to German, and circling his hand around his head. We look at each other and laugh a little...'

The next day, Trotsky relates, at the meeting of the Central Committee, Lenin proposed that Trotsky should be elected chairman of the Soviet of People's Commissars – in other words, head of the new government. 'Why not? You were at the head of the Petrograd Soviet that seized the power.' When Trotsky refused, Lenin suggested that he should be appointed Commissar of Home Affairs. Trotsky feared that his Jewish origin might be a handicap in this position. Lenin impatiently replied: 'We are having a great international revolution. Of what importance are such trifles?' Jacob M. Sverdlov, another Jew, saw the force of Trotsky's objection, and Lenin yielded. The third proposal (suggested by Sverdlov to Lenin), that Trotsky should become the revolution's first Commissar for Foreign Affairs, was readily accepted; and in this capacity, Trotsky found himself reluctantly in charge of the negotiations to secure a peace treaty with the Germans. These took place at Brest Litovsk, a desolate, war-scarred town where the German armies in the East had their headquarters. 'I confess I felt as if I were being led to the torture chamber,' Trotsky wrote. 'Being with strange and alien people always had aroused my fears; it did especially on this occasion.'

When Trotsky arrived at Brest Litovsk on 27 December, preliminary negotiations had been under way for eighteen days. The Russian delegation, headed by Adolf Yoffe, included Kamenev and other leading Bolsheviks as well as a woman Left Social Revolutionary terrorist, A. Vitsenko, who had assassinated a Tsarist Minister of War, General Salcharov. Trotsky was irritated to find his colleagues already on terms of excessive cordiality with the German delegation, which was led by Prince Leopold of Bavaria. What were revolutionaries doing accepting the hospitality of these archetypes of reaction and Imperialism? The Prussian General Hoffman noticed that 'with Trotsky's appearance here, the easy social intercourse outside the conference hall has ceased'.

A Western cartoon, captioned 'That Mischievous Trotsky Boy', at the time of Brest Litovsk
Right: a Civil War poster depicting Trotsky as Saint George slaying the counter-revolutionary dragon.
He was appointed Commissar of War early in 1918

The conclusion of a peace 'equally just to all nations and nationalities without exception' had been the declared aim of Bolshevik foreign policy from the start. The governments of the allied powers, determined to continue the war, had refused to recognize the Soviet régime. Lenin was so confident that revolution was imminent in Germany and other Western countries that he discounted the danger of accepting peace terms dictated by the Germans. Trotsky hoped by entering into peace negotiations 'to arouse the masses of Germany, of Austro-Hungary, as well as of the Entente', but he 'maintained that it was absolutely imperative that we should prove to the workers of Europe . . . how great, how deadly, was our hatred of the rulers of Germany.' On his train journey to Brest Litovsk he had noticed the empty trenches on the Russian side of the front, and realized that he would have to negotiate without the backing of armed strength. As the debates wore on, and the Germans insisted on the continued annexation of Poland and the Baltic states, he also realized that signing the treaty could only bring shameful discredit on the revolution. He returned to Petrograd with a subtle formula which he summed up as: 'we stop the war but do not sign the peace.' Lenin rejected this compromise as unrealistic: 'All this is very attractive and one could wish for nothing better, if only General Hoffman were not strong enough to throw his troops against us . . . You yourself say that our trenches are deserted . . . At the moment there is nothing more important in the world than our revolution; the revolution has to be safeguarded no matter what the price.'

Before returning to Brest Litovsk, Trotsky privately promised Lenin that he would support signing the treaty should the Germans renew military operations. The negotiations continued in an increasingly acrimonious atmosphere. Trotsky made his final speech on 28 January: 'We are withdrawing from the war. We announce this to all peoples and governments. We are issuing an order for the full demobilisation of the army . . . At the same time we declare that the terms proposed to us by the governments of Germany and Austro-Hungary are in fundamental conflict with the interests of all peoples . . . We cannot put the signature of the Russian revolution under a peace treaty which brings oppression, woe and misfortune to millions of human beings.' Back in Petrograd, Trotsky found the Bolshevik party bitterly divided between those supporting Lenin in favour of peace and a majority, led by Bukharin, who were against the treaty. This 'war faction', which was whole-heartedly backed by the Left Social Revolutionaries, assumed from Trotsky's speeches that he was on their side. On 17 February, under Hoffman's orders, the German army launched an offensive which met with no resistance from the disbanded Russian troops; and on the following day Trotsky, true to his promise, cast his deciding vote for Lenin's policy. Shortly afterwards, he resigned from the Commissariat of Foreign Affairs; he was not present when the peace treaty was signed on 3 March 1918.

The Red Guard transformed by Trotsky into the Red Army. Maxim Gorki quotes Lenin as saying: 'Could anyone point out to me another man who would organise an almost model army in a year and win the respect of military experts? We have such a man'

ельский Отдел
музея Республики

ЛЕВ ДАВИДОВИЧ ТРОЦКИЙ,

НАРОДНЫЙ КОМИССАР ПО ВОЕННЫМ и МОРСКИМ ДЕЛАМ. ПРЕДСЕДАТЕЛЬ РЕВОЛЮЦИОННОГО ВОЕННОГО СОВ

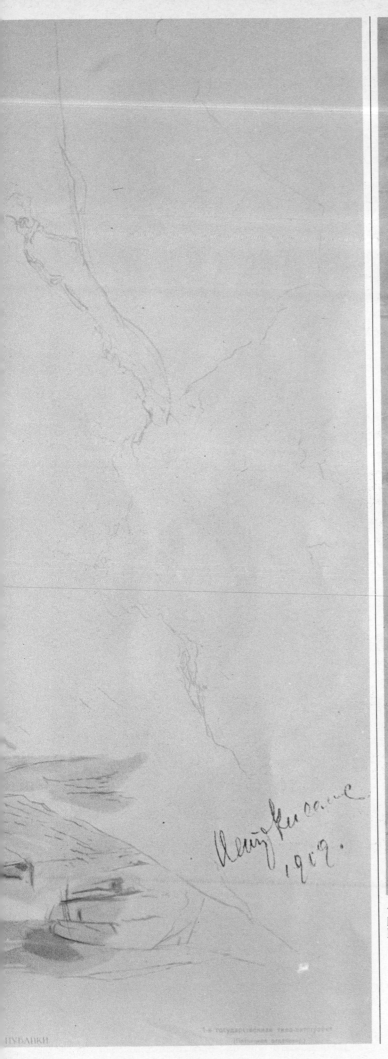

A poster by Mayakovsky exhorting the Red Army to take pride in its appearance
Left: a contemporary drawing of Trotsky at work in 1919

ВСТУПАИТЕ ДО ЧЕРВОНОЇ КІННОТИ!

Червона кіннота знищила Мамонтова, Шкуро, Деникина.
Вона била панів і Петлюру,
    зараз потрібно знищити недобитка Врангеля.
Робітники й селянє—вступайте до лав Червоної Кінноти.

A Red Army recruitment poster. In two years, Trotsky turned seven thousand Red Guards into a fighting force of five million

ЧОРТОВА КУКЛА.

БАРОН
ВРАНГЕЛЬ

№ 121.

Из-за моря, из-за гор
Вылез Врангель живодер
Яро

Эх, армия, не дремли,
Не давай своей земли
Барам

ЛИТЕРАТУРНО-
ИЗДАТЕЛЬСКИЙ
ОТДЕЛА

ПОЛИТУПРАВЛЕНИЯ
Р.В.С.Р.
Сретен бульв д 6

АНТАНТА

ЛЛОЙД ДЖОРДЖ

Д. МООР

Развернулася рука,	На штыке-от глянь, народ	А под буркою сокрыты	Эк их сколько жирных рож.	Мы покуда отдохнем.	Туча черная уйдет.
Двинул красный под бока	Вместо Врангеля урод	Тайна черная бандиты	Мильеран и Джордж и Фош.	А потом и их слихнем	И народное пройдет
Ловко	Головка	Черти.	Ждут смерти	В море	Горе

A Red soldier strips the cloak from Baron Wrangel (see page 71) and exposes the Imperialist conspiracy concealed beneath it

An anti-Semitic White Russian poster depicting Trotsky as the ogre of the Kremlin. When the government moved from Petrograd to Moscow on 12 March, 1918, Trotsky had never been inside the Kremlin and only knew Moscow from the inside of a prison in 1899-1900. 'Lenin and I took quarters across the corridor, sharing the same dining room. The food at the Kremlin was very bad'

Trotsky's next appointment was as Commissar of War, with the formidable task of arming the republic against the combined threat of foreign military intervention and Russian anti-revolutionary forces. The 'peace' had brought nothing but suffering and humiliation to Russia. 'The spring and summer of 1918 were unusually hard', Trotsky wrote in *My Life*. 'One wondered if a country so despairing, so devastated, had enough sap left in it to support a new régime and preserve its independence. There was no food. There was no army. The railways were completely disorganized. The machinery of state was just beginning to take shape. Conspiracies were being hatched everywhere.' The Japanese attacked Siberia and occupied Vladivostok; further menace came from the West. 'The Germans occupied Poland, Lithuania, Latvia, White Russia and a large section of Great Russia . . . The Ukraine became an Austro-German colony. On the Volga, in the summer of 1918, agents of France and England engineered a rebellion of Czechoslovak regiments, made up of former prisoners. The German high command let me know, through their military representatives, that if the Whites approached Moscow from the East, the Germans would come from the West, from the direction of Orsha and Pskov, to prevent the forming of a new eastern front. We were between hammer and anvil. In the North, the French and English occupied Murmansk and Archangel, and threatened an advance on Vologda. In Yaroslavl, there broke out an insurrection of the White Guards, organized by Savinkov at the instigation of the French ambassador Noulens and the English representative Lockhart, with the object of connecting the northern troops with the Czechoslovaks and White Guards on the Volga, by way of Vologda and Yaroslavl. In the Urals, Dutov's bands were at large. In the South, on the Don, an uprising was spreading under the leadership of General Krasnov, then in actual alliance with the Germans. The Left Social Revolutionaries organized a conspiracy in July and murdered Count Mirbach; they tried, at the same time, to start an uprising on the eastern

A map showing the main offensives of the anti-Bolshevik armies in 1919 and 1920. Kolchak was captured by the Czechs, tried and shot in 1920; Denikin escaped to France, emigrated to the U.S.A. in 1945 and died there two years later; Yudenich was arrested by another White Russian General in 1920 but released after Allied intervention and died in England in 1933

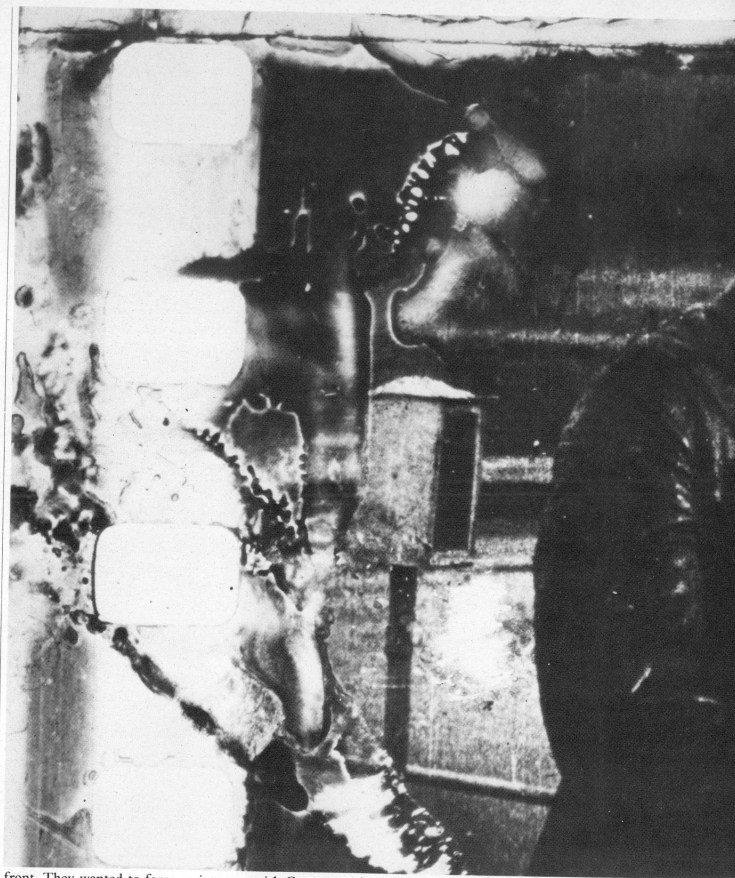

front. They wanted to force us into war with Germany. The civil-war front was taking more and more the shape of a noose closing ever tighter about Moscow.'

Although the White Guards exploited the Jewishness of Trotsky in their propaganda, he found that Lenin had been right about its unimportance in an extreme revolutionary situation. Where anti-semitism existed among the people, it did so in a muddled, ignorant way, reflecting the general confusion of the time. This is recorded in contemporary fiction. Isaac Babel's story *Salt* describes a peasant woman accusing a Red soldier: 'You don't bother your heads about Russia. You just go about saving the dirty Jews, Lenin and Trotsky.' To which he replies: 'I won't say nothing about Lenin, but Trotsky was the desperate son of a governor of Tambov who went over to the working classes . . .' And in *Archives of the Russian Revolution* by V. Seyfulina we find a Cossack saying: 'Trotsky is not a Jew. Trotsky

Trotsky on the Volga during the Civil War

is a fighter. Lenin is a communist and a Jew but Trotsky is Russian, one of us.' As a Marxist and enemy of all forms of religion, Trotsky had no feeling for the Jewish faith; in fact, while the Ukraine was occupied by the Germans in 1918, the rabbis of Odessa pronounced anathema on both Trotsky and Zinoviev.

Trotsky was now installed in the Kremlin with Natalya and their two sons; his first wife, Alexandra, was living at Petrograd with his daughters. Alexandra had remained an active revolutionary: she is described, some years later, by Victor Serge as 'plump, her hair white over her kindly face . . . the last word in commonsense and honesty . . . I have known few Marxists as free in their basic outlook as Alexandra Lvovna.' Natalya, whose interests had always been more artistic than political, worked for the Commissariat of Education and was put in charge of the preservation of museums and ancient

Trotsky in one of the cars which travelled on his train. Right: a montage of Trotsky directing operations on the various fronts

monuments. This was a difficult task during a civil war. 'Neither the White nor the Red troops were much inclined to look out for historical estates, provincial Kremlins or ancient churches', Trotsky writes. 'This led to many arguments between the war commissariat and the department of museums. The guardians of the palaces and churches accused the troops of lack of respect for culture; the military commissars accused the guardians of preferring dead objects to living people. Formally, it looked as if I were engaged in an endless departmental quarrel with my wife. Many jokes were made about us on this score.'

Neither of Trotsky's families saw much of him during the two and a half years of the civil war. On one of his short visits to Moscow, Trotsky suggested to Lenin that, considering the bad situation in the Urals, the Tsar should be tried in open court as the proceedings would reveal to the people the corruption of his whole reign. Lenin replied that this would be good if it were feasible, but there might not be enough time. The next time that Trotsky left the front for Moscow, in July 1918, he asked Sverdlov in passing: 'And where is the Tsar?' Sverdlov told him that all the Imperial family had been shot: 'Ivan Ilyich believed that we shouldn't leave the Whites a live banner to rally around, especially under the present difficult circumstances.' Trotsky later wrote that he considered Lenin's decision 'not only expedient but necessary'.

On 6 August 1918, the Red Army retreated from Simbirsk and Kazan, on the eastern bank of the upper Volga, before the advance of the Czechoslovak Legion and the White Guards under Admiral Kolchak. Once the enemy had crossed the river, only an open plain would have separated them from Moscow. Trotsky travelled to Svyazhsk, a small town opposite Kazan on the western bank. He was there when a Social Revolutionary, Fanya Kaplan, made an attempt to assassinate Lenin in Moscow, and another Social Revolutionary, Leonid Kanegiesser, succeeded in killing Moses Uritsky at Petrograd. Uritsky worked for the Cheka – the Extraordinary Commission for Struggle against Counter-revolution which was later known as the GPU. These acts of defiance unleashed a Red Terror far worse than any repressive measures the Cheka had taken before.

Trotsky's exploits at Svyazhsk are described by Isaac Deutscher in *The Prophet Armed*: 'He found the front in a state of virtual collapse...From his train, which stood within reach of enemy fire, he descended into panic-stricken crowds of soldiers, poured out on them torrents of passionate eloquence . . . and personally led them back to the fighting line...The local commissars proposed that he should move to a safer place on a steamboat on the Volga; but fearing the effect this might have on the troops, he refused. On a ramshackle torpedo boat he went with sailors of Kronstadt, who had brought over a tiny flotilla to the Volga, on an adventurous night raid to

Поварищ Троцкий

Kazan. Most of the flotilla was destroyed but it managed to silence the enemy batteries on the banks of the river; and Trotsky returned safely to his base.'

Trotsky's train had been hastily assembled in Moscow on the night of 7 August in order to take him to Svyazshk. From that date, he virtually lived in it for over two years throughout the civil war, travelling along the twenty-one fronts held by the fourteen armies under his command. It became a tangible symbol of the embattled revolution, and ultimately of victory. 'The train was continually being reorganized and improved upon [he writes]. Its sections included a secretariat, a printing-press, a telegraph station, a radio station, an electric power station, a library, a garage and a bath. The train

Red soldiers on one of the armoured trains which engaged in bombardment throughout the Civil War
Left: E. M. Sklyansky, Trotsky's deputy, a young army doctor who presided over the Revolutionary Military Council while Trotsky was away from Moscow
Top Left: Trotsky outside the train of the Chairman of the Revolutionary Military Council

was so heavy that it needed two engines; later it was divided into two trains. When we had to stop for some time at some one section of the front, one of the engines would do service as courier, and the other was always under steam . . . Part of the train was a huge garage holding several automobiles and a petrol tank. This made it possible for us to travel away from the railway line for several hundred miles. A squad of picked sharpshooters

and machine-gunners, amounting to from twenty to thirty men, occupied the trucks and light cars. A couple of hand machine-guns had also been placed in my car ... The train was not only a military-administrative and political institution, but a fighting institution as well.'

A detailed description of the train is to be found in *Lenin's Moscow*, by Alfred Rosmer, who came to Russia in 1920: 'The coach of the People's Commissar had belonged to the Tsarist Minister of Railways, and Trotsky had adapted it for his use. The lounge had been transformed into an office-cum-library. The other part consisted of the bathroom, with a narrow room on each side of it with just enough space for a divan. The following coach was for the secretaries; then followed in turn the printing-press, the library, the recreation room, the restaurant, a coach for provisions and spare clothing, an ambulance service, and finally a coach specially fitted for the two motor-cars ... At all times the train was a hive of activity. There was a newspaper which appeared daily with leaders, a commentary on events, and the "latest news". At the appropriate times, the radio would pick up foreign broadcasts. "Your French radio is completely stupid," Trotsky said to me: "Berlin and London give interesting news, but your radio is nothing but rubbish." Trotsky always had some work in preparation, and when military operations permitted, he would set his secretaries to work, dictating and revising the typed sheets ... No one made greater demands on

Trotsky and 'the train of the Predrevoyensoviet' visiting the Western Front in 1918. 'My own personal life was inseparably boun

up with the life of that train', he wrote. 'The train, on the other hand, was inseparably bound up with the life of the Red Army'

himself than Trotsky. He had a horror of carelessness of style, just as in dress and behaviour. He would go over the dictated pages again, reread them, correct them, rearrange them; a second and a third copying became necessary . . . The work-table was almost the whole of one side, on the wall of which hung a huge map of Russia. On the two walls at right angles to this were book-shelves weighed down with books . . . I was very surprised to see Mallarmé's *Verse and Prose Works* . . .'

Trotsky's plan for transforming the undisciplined Red Guards at his disposal into leaders of an efficient fighting force drawn from the untrained Russian masses had necessitated a complex scheme of rigid centralization which exploited the valuable experience of former Tsarist officers. This had been severely criticized from the start, by Zinoviev and many others who considered that

Trotsky addresses the troops from the top of an armoured train called 'Guard of the Revolution'
Right: Trotsky with General S. Kamenev during the Civil War
Top: Stalin at the Tsaritsin front in the summer of 1918

any form of military hierarchy was not only undemocratic but essentially counter-revolutionary as well. The Svyazhsk engagement, however, was a conspicuous success: the Reds recaptured Kazan and Simbirsk in September 1919, and by October the whole of the Volga region had been regained. Trotsky returned to Moscow to set up and control a Revolutionary War Council of the Republic. The White Guards were now strongest on the southern front, where Voroshilov's Tenth Army had its headquarters at Tsaritsin and where Joseph Stalin was the chief political commissar. (Tsaritsin was later re-named Stalingrad.) When Trotsky ordered the re-organization of this front, Stalin supported Voroshilov in resisting all reforms. Trotsky had both Stalin and Voroshilov replaced by other men. The 'Tsaritsin group' revenged itself by a whispering campaign, accusing Trotsky of persecuting Bolsheviks in the army and of the indiscriminate execution of local commissars. (One commissar, Panteleev, had in fact been court-martialled for desertion and shot at Svyazhsk.) Stalin and Zinoviev between them tried to put Lenin against Trotsky, apparently with some success – although Maxim Gorki quotes Lenin as saying: 'Too many lies are being told, and especially about me and Trotsky.'

In the spring of 1919, Admiral Kolchak renewed his offensive against the Volga and Moscow, and was repulsed by General S. Kamenev, a former colonel in the Tsarist army. Kamenev wished to pursue Kolchak into Siberia, but Trotsky considered this dangerous and, after an argument on the subject, removed Kamenev from his command. S. I. Gusev and other commissars in the eastern front complained to Stalin and Lenin, with

the result that Trotsky's decision was reversed; he was proved to have been wrong when Kamenev eventually succeeded in smashing Kolchak's forces in Siberia. Trotsky spent the summer on the southern front, where General Denikin, also aiming at Moscow, had advanced into the Ukraine and seized Tsaritsin and Kharkov. Once more, Trotsky came into conflict with General Kamenev, who wanted the main force of the Red Army to be concentrated on the eastern sector, along the Don valley, while Trotsky thought it should be shifted to the centre; and once more, Trotsky was overruled. On this occasion, he was to be proved right – but it was not until October, when Denikin's troops were nearly at Moscow, that the Politbureau had to acknowledge their mistake in backing Kamenev's plan rather than his.

A large part of the Ukraine was controlled by a guerrilla leader, Nestor I. Makhno, and his 'Ukrainian Army of Insurgent Peasants'. This picturesque group of anarchists fought under a black flag; they attacked the Whites, but also resisted the Reds. Victor Serge gives a romantic description of Makhno in *Memoirs of a Revolutionary*: 'boozing, swashbuckling, disorderly and idealistic . . . Makhno invented a form of infantry mounted in carts, which gave him enormous mobility. He also invented the procedure of burying his weapons and disbanding his forces for a while. His men would pass, unarmed, through the front lines, unearth a new supply of machine-guns from another spot, and spring up again in an unexpected quarter.' Of peasant stock, Makhno had been first a shepherd and then an industrial worker. He had taken part in the 1905 revolution, after which he became an anarchist. Arrested in 1908, he had

Nestor Makhno with his Ukrainian Army
Right: Admiral Kolchak
Above right: General Denikin

left the Butyrsky prison in Moscow during the February revolution and returned to his home in the Ukraine to found his Black Army. This consisted of some 15000 soldiers in September 1919, when he inflicted a significant defeat on Denikin at Uman. Despite their disapproval of anarchism, Lenin and Trotsky later considered recognizing an autonomous region for Makhno and his followers; and in October 1920, a treaty of alliance with Makhno was signed, on behalf of the Red Army, by Bela Kun, S. I. Gusev and M. V. Frunze. But shortly afterwards, when their victory had been assured, the Bolshevik leaders revoked the treaty, and Makhno's forces were dispersed by the same Red Army which had profited from their bravery throughout the war. Makhno, surrounded, escaped with some of his troops and continued to fight on desperately until August 1921: he finally fled to Rumania, and ended his life as a factory-worker in Paris.

By the beginning of October 1919, it looked as if the Red Army had lost the civil war. Denikin, after successively capturing Kiev, Kursk, Voronezh and Orel, was almost at Tula, the last important town before Moscow. At the same time, General N. Yudenich, armed by the British, had advanced from Estonia and was on the outskirts of Petrograd. The crisis was so acute that Lenin was even prepared to abandon Petrograd altogether and mass every available force in an attempt to save Moscow. Trotsky – for once supported by Stalin – was vigorously opposed to any plan involving the surrender of Petrograd.

He volunteered to go there himself and take charge of its defence. At Petrograd, Trotsky found British tanks already in the suburbs and the city in a panic. Summoning all his energy and powers of persuasion, he rallied troops and civilians alike; within a week of his arrival, they had beaten back the enemy and taken the offensive themselves. On 26 October, his fortieth birthday and the revolution's second anniversary, he returned to Moscow with the news of victory. Meanwhile, in the south, General Semyen Budenny's Red Cavalry had driven Denikin back to the Don, and Moscow was safe. Throughout that terrible summer, the Soviet régime, menaced from abroad and divided within itself, had been in the gravest danger, while Trotsky's personal fortunes had appeared to be at their lowest ebb. Now suddenly, as the acknowledged architect of a triumphant military victory, he was at the summit of his political career; and the revolution, having defied intervention from outside and defeated rebellion from within, seemed secure at last. In January 1920, the Entente lifted its blockade from Russia: the sinister powers of the Cheka were curtailed, and the death penalty was abolished.

The apparent end to the civil conflict, however, proved to be delusory: soon the Bolsheviks found themselves engaged in their first national war. At the beginning of April the Polish army, under Joseph Pilsudski, marched into the Ukraine; and Trotsky prepared to deal the invaders 'a blow which would resound in the streets of Warsaw and throughout the world'. By June, Kiev had been recaptured by the Russians and Pilsudski's troops had been pushed back to the Polish border. Lenin was anxious that the Red Army should continue its advance to Warsaw and beyond; to this, Trotsky was resolutely opposed. But Lenin was supported by the whole of the Politbureau – with the exception of Alexei Rykov, who briefly took Trotsky's side. Meanwhile, the interventionist party in Britain, led by Winston Churchill, had been considerably weakened by the Bolshevik successes; and in July the Foreign Secretary, Lord Curzon, offered British mediation between Russia and Poland. Trotsky was in favour of accepting this proposal, but Lenin insisted on his rejecting it. 'In contrast to the Brest Litovsk period,' Trotsky wrote, 'the roles had been completely reversed. Then it was I who demanded that the signing of the peace be delayed; that even at the price of losing some territory, we give the German proletariat time to understand the situation and get in its word. Now it was Lenin who demanded that our army continue its advance and give the Polish proletariat time to appraise the situation and rise up in arms.' The march on Warsaw turned out to be as great a disaster as Brest Litovsk: in both cases, Trotsky wrote, 'we passed over and beyond our own victory to a heavy defeat.' Lenin, his gaze fixed on international revolution, had misjudged the temper of the Polish peasants and workers, who viewed the Russian soldiers as invaders rather than as liberators. The Red Army had reached the outskirts of Warsaw by the beginning of August; but after the Battle of the

Vistula, which lasted only three days, it was decisively beaten and forced to retreat in disorder. Lenin's misguided attempt to 'carry the revolution abroad on the point of bayonets' had failed.

While the Red Army was tied down by the Poles, the remnants of Denikin's White Guards had reassembled under Baron Petr Wrangel in the Crimea and had invaded the Caucasus. Shortly after the Soviets had signed a provisional peace with Pilsudski's Poland, Trotsky set off for the Crimea to prepare an offensive against Wrangel. He wrote in his train newspaper, *En Route*, on 27 October 1920: 'Our train is again bound for the front. The fighting men of our train went before the walls of Kazan in the grave weeks of 1918, when we were fighting for control of the Volga. That fight ended long ago. Today the Soviet

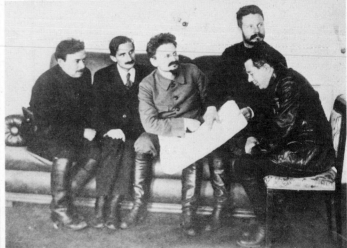

In conference during the Civil War: left to right, Bela Kun, Alfred Rosmer, Trotsky, M. V. Frunze and S. I. Gusev
Above: Trotsky with troops at the Polish front
Left: Baron Petr Wrangel
Above left: Red Army troops advancing against the Whites

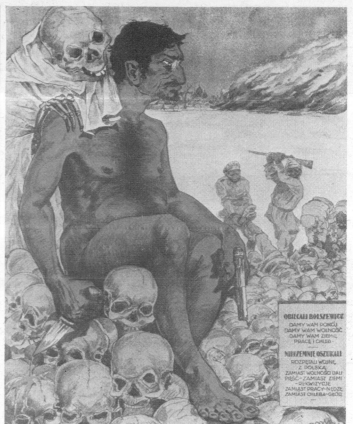

More anti-Semitic propaganda: a Polish attack on Trotsky
Left: Trotsky addresses the troops before they leave for
the Polish front to fight Pilsudski
Overleaf: Lenin and Trotsky at the Second Congress of the
Third International in 1920

power is approaching the Pacific Ocean. The fighting men of our train fought gallantly before the walls of Petrograd. Petrograd has been saved and has since been visited by representatives of the world proletariat. Our train visited the Western front more than once. Today, a preliminary peace has been signed with Poland. The fighting men of our train were on the steppes of the Don when Krasnov and, later, Denikin advanced against Soviet Russia from the South. The days of Krasnov and Denikin are long since past. There now is left only the Crimea, which the French government has made its fortress. The White Guard garrison of this French fortress is under the command of a hired German-Russian general, Baron Wrangel. The friendly family of our train is starting on a new campaign. Let this campaign be the last.' The Crimean campaign was indeed the last of the civil war. After a savage battle, the Red Army drove Wrangel into the sea; and a few months later Trotsky's train was disbanded.

David Bronstein had had a difficult time throughout the civil war, persecuted both by the Whites because he was Trotsky's father and by the Reds because he was a *kulak* – that is, a rich, land-owning peasant. At the age of seventy, having lost all his money, he decided to seek out his son: he travelled several hundred miles on foot, through battle-ridden territory, from his home to Odessa, finally reaching Moscow in 1920. Trotsky found him a job as manager of a state mill just outside the city. The old man worked happily and hard, making a success of the mill until his death from typhus two years later.

Trotsky and Lenin had been calling for the formation of a Third Communist International (or Comintern) since 1914. It came into being in March 1919, with Zinoviev as its President in Petrograd but rigidly controlled by Lenin from the Kremlin. 'The Third International took over the work of the Second International, cut off its opportunistic, bourgeois and petit-bourgeois rubbish, and began to carry into effect the dictatorship of the proletariat,' Lenin wrote. 'Soviet or proletarian democracy was born in Russia . . . Soviet republics in countries with a higher degree of civilization, whose proletariat has greater social weight and influence, have every prospect of outstripping Russia as soon as they start upon the road of proletarian dictatorship.' Like Trotsky, Lenin was convinced that the Soviet régime would not survive unless it inspired a chain reaction of revolutions in other parts of Europe, and that socialism in one country could never be a success. But he had formed the Comintern at an unpropitious moment. Already, in January 1919, the Spartacist uprising in Berlin had been suppressed, and Karl Liebknecht and Rosa Luxemburg had been killed. In March of the same year, Hungary became a Soviet Republic under Bela Kun, and in April Munich also acquired a Soviet régime; but Bela Kun's dictatorship, which was unpopular with most of the Hungarian people, did not last more than several months, while Munich fell to General Hoffman after only a few weeks. None of these reverses had shaken

Eleven Bolshevik leaders, with Lenin in the centre and Trotsky and Stalin above him
Top: Trotsky, Lenin and L. B. Kamenev in discussion during the Second Congress
Above right: Lenin, Mikhail I. Kalinin (President of the Soviet Republic) and Trotsky

Lenin's confidence when he ordered the ill-fated march on Warsaw, which he did during the Second Congress of the Third International at Moscow in 1920. Meanwhile, to counter the threats posed by Pilsudski and Wrangel, the revolution had reverted to the use of terror. The sinister Cheka grew powerful again, and the death penalty was restored: in July 1920, 800 men were executed by military tribunals alone. These developments were severely criticized by anti-Bolshevik socialists abroad, in particular by Martov and the German Social Democrat Karl Kautsky. Trotsky replied to Kautsky in a pamphlet, *Terrorism and Communism*, written in 1920:

'If our revolution had taken place a few months, or even a few weeks, after the establishment of the rule of the proletariat in Germany, France and England, there can be no doubt that our revolution would have been the most "peaceful", the most "bloodless" of all possible revolutions on this sinful earth. But this historical sequence – the most "natural" at the first glance, and, in any case, the most beneficial for the Russian working class – found itself infringed – not through our fault, but through the will of events. Instead of being the last, the Russian proletariat proved to be the first. It was just this circumstance, after the first period of confusion, that imparted desperation to the character of the resistance of the classes which had ruled in Russia previously, and forced the Russian proletariat, in a moment of the greatest peril, foreign attacks, and internal plots and insurrections, to have recourse to severe measures of State terror...

'The revolution "logically" does not demand terrorism...But the revolution does require of the revolutionary class that it should attain its end by all methods at its disposal – if necessary, by an armed rising; if required, by terrorism. "But, in that case, in what do your tactics differ from the tactics of Tsarism?" we are asked by the high priests of Liberalism and Kautskianism. You do not understand this, holy men? We shall explain to you. The terror of Tsarism was directed against the proletariat. The gendarmerie of Tsarism throttled the workers who were fighting for the socialist order. Our Extraordinary Commissions shoot landlords, capitalists, and generals who are striving to restore the capitalist order. Do you grasp this distinction? Yes? For us communists it is quite sufficient...'

Since their rapprochement in 1917, Trotsky and Lenin had differed in their opinions about the peace of Brest Litovsk and the invasion of Poland. At the end of 1920, they found themselves in disagreement for the third time. 'One cannot deny that the so-called discussion of trades unions clouded our relationship,' Trotsky writes. 'Each of us was too much the revolutionary and too much the politician to be able or even to want to separate the personal from the general. It was during that discussion that Stalin and Zinoviev were given what one might call their legal opportunity to bring their struggle against me out into the open . . . But it was just this aspect of the thing that disturbed Lenin most, and he tried in every way to paralyse it.'

As before, Trotsky's position in the new debate was extremely complex. Russia was faced with the problem of finding some alternative to the 'war communism' which had been necessitated by the civil war and which involved the requisitioning of food from the peasants. In January 1920, Lenin and Trotsky had proposed the militarization of civilian labour ('He who does not work shall not eat') which had been indignantly rejected by the Bolshevik trade-union leaders. Trotsky then supervised the transformation of the armies of the Urals, the Caucasus and the Ukraine into a labour force. During a tour of inspection in the Urals, the apathy of the people was brought home to him, and he came to the conclusion that war communism must be abandoned. 'My practical work had satisfied me that the methods of war communism forced on us by the conditions of civil war were completely exhausted, and that to revive our economic life the element of personal interest must be introduced at all costs; in other words, we had to restore the home

Trotsky with his son Sergei Sedov in 1920
Right: Trotsky being filmed while making a speech in Moscow

market in some degree. I submitted to the Central Committee the project of replacing the food levy by a grain-tax and of restoring the exchange of commodities.' Requisitioning would cease: having paid his tax, the peasant would be free to dispose of his crop as he chose. In February 1920, Lenin came out firmly against these proposals – which could be said to imply a modified revival of private trade – although they were basically identical to those incorporated in the New Economic Policy which he brought in a year later. Instead of persis-

ting in his plan, Trotsky met Lenin's rebuff by a complete change of front. If war communism had to continue, he decided, then it must be made to work. 'When the change to the market system was rejected, I demanded that the "war" methods be applied properly and with system, so that real economic improvements could be maintained. In the system of war communism in which all the resources are, at least in principle, nationalized and distributed by the government order, I saw no independent role for trades unions. If industry rests on the state's insuring the supply of all the necessary products to the workers, the trades unions must be included in the system of the state's administration of industry and distribution of products.'

The bold and intransigent logic of Trotsky's reasoning – which illustrated both the strength of his intellect and the weakness of his judgement – seemed to have led him first to countenance a form of capitalism, however tentative, and then to attack the machinery of proletarian democracy. If the reforms he had suggested in February came too soon for Lenin, these stern measures which he advocated in December definitely came too late. Lenin easily persuaded the Central Committee to reject them – and continued with his own preparations for the New Economic Policy which he successfully launched at the Tenth Congress of the Bolshevik Party in March 1921. Trotsky's attempt to undermine the independence of the trades unions had given ammunition to the Workers' Opposition, led by A. G. Shliapnikov and Alexandra Kollontai, which resisted Lenin's dictatorship and was the first group of Bolshevik dissenters to diagnose the early symptoms of bureaucratic privilege in the Soviet state. Trotsky continued his assault in a speech at the Congress: 'The Workers' Opposition has come out with dangerous slogans. They have made a fetish of democratic principles. They have placed the workers' right to elect representatives above the party, as it were, as if the party were not entitled to assert its dictatorship even if that dictatorship temporarily clashed with the passing moods of the workers' democracy . . . The party is obliged to maintain its dictatorship, regardless of temporary vacillations even in the working class.' Lenin resisted the extreme changes demanded by Trotsky. Instead he proposed resolutions whereby the trades unions would retain a degree of autonomy – and these were accepted by an overwhelming majority at the Congress.

Trotsky was in an isolated position – worse, he was in a position which seemed to contradict his essential beliefs and many of his past (and future) pronouncements. Once he had written, in an attack on the 'Jacobinism' of Lenin, 'a proletariat capable of exercising its authority over society will not tolerate any dictatorship over itself.' Now he had become the spokesman for the extreme 'Jacobin' idea of substituting the dictatorship of the Party for the will of the working class. Yet, as Isaac Deutscher writes, 'even his denial of principle was still dictated by principle . . . The very absurdity of his behaviour contained its own antidote. In his candour he

gave the people ample notice of the danger threatening them. He indicated the limits to which he was prepared to go. He submitted his policies to public control. He himself did everything in his power to provoke the resistance that frustrated him.'

Trotsky later paid tribute to 'the unerring political instinct' of Lenin at this time. 'Whereas I was trying to get an ever more intensive effort from the trades unions, taking my stand on purely economic considerations on the basis of war communism, Lenin, guided by political considerations, was moving towards an easing of the military pressure.' When Lenin announced the first, guarded stages in the change to the New Economic Policy, Trotsky subscribed to them at once: 'For me, they were merely a renewal of the proposals which I had introduced a year before. The dispute about the trades unions instantly lost all significance. Lenin took no part in that dispute, and left Zinoviev to amuse himself with the shell of an exploded cartridge . . . And it was only a few months later that Lenin formulated entirely new principles on the role and purpose of trades unions, based on the new economic policy. I expressed my unreserved approval of his resolution. Our solid front was restored. Lenin was afraid that as a result of the discussion . . . permanent factions would be established in the party, embittering relationships and making the work much more difficult.' As in all their previous disputes, the difference between Lenin and Trotsky was essentially a question of timing. Both men reached identical conclusions but through separate processes of thought, and although they invariably met at the same point in the end, they did not always arrive there at the same moment.

Above and left: two pictures of Trotsky in Red Square
Top: portrait of Trotsky in 1920
Above left: Trotsky with Alexei Rykov and one of Trotsky's aides, I. Impazmin
Overleaf: Trotsky speaking in Red Square, 1920

A solid front was more than ever necessary for the Bolsheviks now. The preliminaries of the Tenth Party Congress had been brutally interrupted, at the end of February 1921, by disturbing news from Kronstadt – the naval base established on an island in the Gulf of Finland twenty miles west of Petrograd. The Kronstadt sailors had a record of hot-headed revolutionary zeal. They had mutinied in 1905, and again the following year. In May 1917, impatient with the Provisional Government, they had proclaimed: 'The sole power in Kronstadt is the Soviet of Workers' and Soldiers' Deputies.' Trotsky writes of them in his *History of the Russian Revolution*: 'Tempered in the terrible régime of the Tsarist fleet and the naval fortress, accustomed to stern work, to sacrifices, but also to fury, these sailors, now when the curtain of the new life was beginning to rise before them, a life in which they felt themselves to be the coming masters, tightened all their sinews in order to prove themselves worthy of the revolution . . . The Kronstadt sailors became a kind of fighting crusaders of the revolution.' When they were tried by the Petrograd Soviet on 27 May 1917, Trotsky had appeared in their defence, warning that 'when a counter-revolutionary general tries to throw a noose around the neck of the revolution . . . the Kronstadt sailors will come to fight and die with us.' Sure enough, the sailors had helped put down Kornilov in August; and in October they had led the storming of the Winter Palace. Trotsky's admiration for them was returned: they almost idolized him. Now he heard that they had rebelled once more – but, this time, against Lenin's government.

The Bolsheviks (as they had done with Makhno and other dissident anarchist movements) made out that the sailors were in league with the Whites, under a mythical General Kozlovsky. The truth seems to be that they had mutinied independently, after the Kronstadt Soviet had published a programme for the 'renewal of the Revolution'. Its contents are summarized by Victor Serge: 're-election of the Soviets by secret ballot; freedom of the spoken and printed word for all revolutionary parties and groupings; freedom for the trades unions; the release of revolutionary political prisoners; abolition of political propaganda; an end to requisitioning in the countryside; freedom for the artisan class; immediate suppression of the barrier squads that were stopping the people from getting their food as they pleased.' When Mikhail I. Kalinin, the President of the Republic's Executive, visited the Kronstadt garrison, he was wel-

Red Army machine-gunners firing on the Kronstadt sailors. Right: Trotsky in 1921

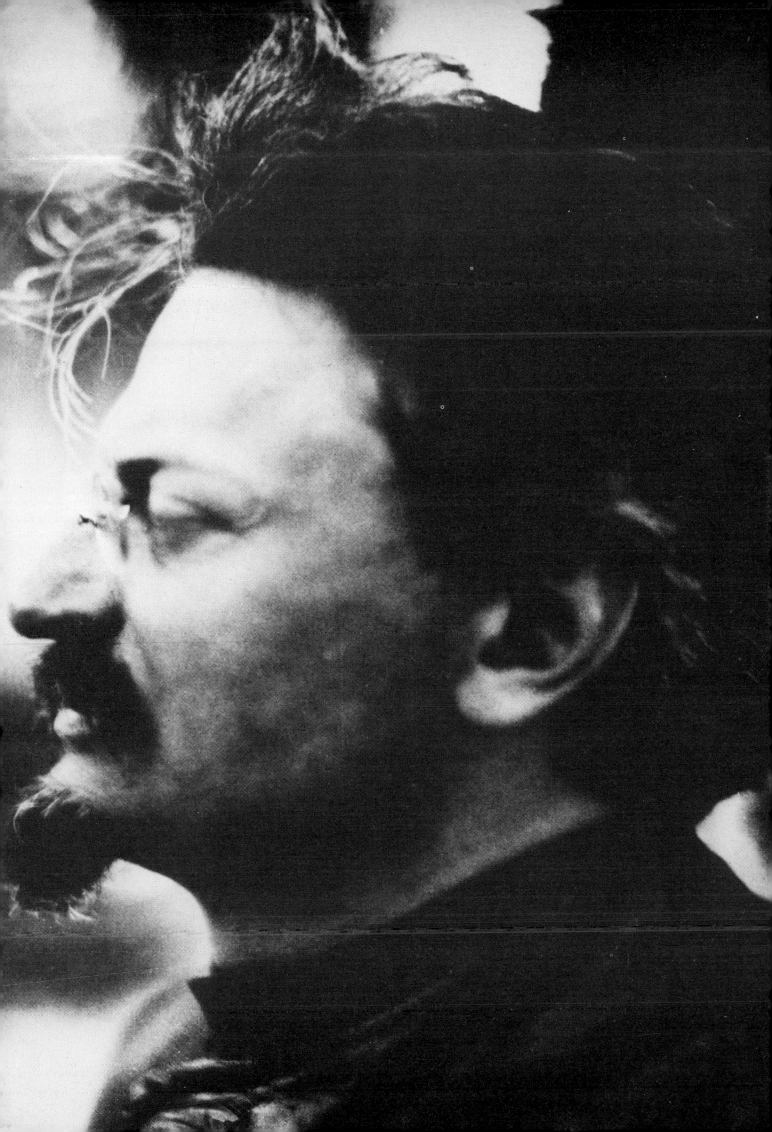

comed with music and salutes; but after he had heard the sailors' demands, he treated them as treacherous riff-raff who were only out for themselves, and threatened them with merciless reprisals. Serge suggests that it was Kalinin who invented the 'White General Kozlovsky' on his return to Petrograd; certainly, it was Kalinin's bungling of the situation that provoked the rising. Once it had started, all the enemies of the Bolsheviks – Left and Right Social Revolutionaries, Anarchists, Mensheviks – hurried to join in, while the foreign press exulted. A Social Revolutionary, V.M. Chernov, inflamed the situation by warning the rebels: 'Don't let yourselves be deceived by engaging in negotiations with the Bolshevik authorities; they are doing it only in order to gain time.' It is an ironic historical fact that, during the disturbances in July 1917, Chernov had been seized by the angry Kronstadt sailors and his release had only been secured through Trotsky's intervention. Now, they (or their younger brothers) listened to Chernov rather than to Trotsky, when the latter warned them on 5 March that only those rebels who surrendered unconditionally could 'count on the mercy of the Soviet Republic'. If the sailors could hold out until the thaw set in, opening supply routes from Finland to their armed but ice-bound fortress, they would become almost invincible. General Tukhachevsky decided to seize the fortress before this could happen. Isaac Deutscher describes the dramatic assault: 'White sheets over their uniforms, the Bolshevik troops, under Tukhachevsky's command, advanced across the bay. They were met by hurricane fire from Kronstadt's

bastions. The ice broke under their feet; and wave after wave of white-shrouded attackers collapsed into the glacial Valhalla. The death march went on . . . On March 17, after a night-long advance in a snow-storm, the Bolsheviks at last succeeded in climbing the walls. When they broke into the fortress, they fell upon its defenders like revengeful furies.' This fury was sustained in savage reprisals after the suppression of the revolt.

The Kronstadt rising had a quality of nightmare not only for the slaughtered sailors but also for the Bolsheviks who so ruthlessly repressed them. It was as if the spirit of October 1917 had risen, after little more than three years, to reproach its leaders with having asserted the dictatorship of the Party over the proletariat at the very moment when they were reluctantly retreating

A Russian soldier shot while crossing the ice at Kronstadt
Right: Gregory Y. Zinoviev

Lenin and Trotsky in Petrograd at the centre of a group of soldiers who had taken part in the suppression of the Kronstadt rising

from war communism into the compromise of the New Economic Policy. Kronstadt became a symbol of the dilemma with which a revolutionary government is faced once it has achieved power and finds itself defending the status quo in an apparently revolutionary situation. A paragraph in Trotsky's posthumously published *Stalin* shows that he saw the political aspect of the incident in straightforward terms: 'What the Soviet government did reluctantly at Kronstadt was a tragic necessity; naturally, the revolutionary government could not have "presented" the fortress that protected Petrograd to the insurgent sailors only because a few dubious Anarchists and Social Revolutionaries were sponsoring a handful of reactionary peasants and soldiers in rebellion.' But the accusing ghost of Kronstadt refused to be laid by logic alone; and throughout the last twenty years of Trotsky's life, which were devoted to exposing and explaining the crimes of Stalin and the Soviet bureaucracy, the episode was repeatedly invoked as evidence against his own integrity. Critics from almost every political standpoint used it to imply that Lenin and Trotsky had already sown, in 1921, the seeds of Stalin's later abuses. It was not until July 1938, that Trotsky felt called upon to clarify the extent of his personal responsibility in the affair. 'The truth of the matter,' he wrote then, 'is that *I personally did not participate in the least in the suppression of the Kronstadt rebellion, nor in the following repressions . . .* The decision to suppress the rebellion by military force, *if the fortress could not be induced to surrender, first by peace negotiations, then through an ultimatum* – this general decision was adopted with my direct participation. But after the decision was taken, I continued to remain in Moscow and took no part, direct or indirect, in the military operations. Concerning the subsequent repressions, they were completely the affair of the Cheka . . . The political work in Kronstadt was wholly in the hands of the Petrograd committee, at the head of which stood Zinoviev.' Zinoviev had recently been Trotsky's most passionate opponent in the trades unions debate, and the sailors who took part in the rebellion had (not surprisingly) supported Zinoviev over this. Trotsky explains that he had therefore deliberately absented himself from Kronstadt, for fear that the sailors might interpret his participation as a form of personal revenge. He insists, however, that this disclaimer is beside the point. 'Idealists and pacifists always accused the revolution of "excesses". But the main point is that "excesses" flow from the very nature of revolution which in itself is but an "excess" of history. Whoever so desires may on this basis reject revolution in general. I do not reject it. In this sense I carry full and complete responsibility for the suppression of the Kronstadt rebellion.'

Downfall 1921-1929

Trotsky in Moscow on the fifth anniversary of the October revolution

In the spring of 1921, the Russian people had already endured seven years of world war, revolution, civil war, war of intervention and war communism: now they were threatened by the apocalyptic spectre of famine. Shortly after the Kronstadt rising, alarming reports reached Moscow of drought, blizzards and a plague of locusts in the southern and south-eastern regions of the Volga. By the end of the year, 36,000,000 peasants were suffering from the famine – either

dead from starvation or, displaced from their homes by the blizzards and the locusts, wandering aimlessly over the plains in such extremity that some were even driven to cannibalism. Faced by this desperate situation, the Bolshevik government abandoned its proud principles and appealed to foreign charity for help: relief on a large scale was distributed by an American organization under Herbert Hoover. During another famine, in 1892, Lenin had attacked sentimental humanitarianism and insisted that the famine was 'the direct consequence of a particular social order. So long as that order exists, famines are inevitable. They can be abolished only by the abolition of that order of society.'

Trotsky's peculiar gifts stemmed from his temperament: his high sense of drama, which contrasted so sharply with Lenin's unobtrusive personality, had made a romantic appeal to the Russian people and inspired them to great acts of courage and self-sacrifice. This magnetism had ideally fitted him for the Herculean task of leading the revolution through its initial crisis, as long as its existence was endangered by reactionary forces inside the country and armed intervention from abroad. Once the civil war had been won, however, the heroic age of the new régime was past. No more revolutionary zeal could be demanded of a population enfeebled by hunger, and little glamour attached to the inauguration of the New Economic Policy. At the beginning of 1922, the army had been reduced to a third of its former size and the Commissariat of War was no longer the hub of the government; as its head, Trotsky found his powers under-extended. He applied his energies to formulating the complex details of the New Economic Policy and gave more of his time than before to the Communist International. He also assumed numerous other duties, including the leadership of the Society of the Godless, which was responsible for the dissemination of anti-religious propaganda. But his imaginative brilliance, given free rein in war, was restricted by the bureaucratic routine which emerged with peace, and to which the more pedestrian but more devious methods employed by Stalin seemed to be perfectly suited.

During the Eleventh Party Congress in March 1922, Zinoviev proposed that Stalin should fill the newly created post of General Secretary of the Central Committee of the All-Russian Communist Party. Lenin was dubious ('This cook will only serve peppery dishes,' he said of Stalin to Trotsky) but he eventually approved the appointment. Perhaps to allay his misgivings, Lenin invited Trotsky in April to become a deputy Chairman of the Council of People's Commissars. Trotsky haughtily refused. The position would have nominally established him as Lenin's second in command – but two other men, Rykov and A. Tsurupa, already held this title, and it was later offered to Kamenev as well. Trotsky may have felt that, under these circumstances, his unofficial standing as Lenin's deputy did not need formal recognition; but if Trotsky was slightly insulted by the offer, Lenin was hurt and angry when it was declined. Nobody then attached much importance to the role of Stalin as General Secretary, which as long as Lenin lived had only a technical character and no political significance; and although Lenin had been suffering from headaches and insomnia for several months, his good health and long life seem to have been taken for granted.

One Sunday early in May, Trotsky went fishing with a net in the old channel of the Moscow river. He slipped on the wet grass, hurt his foot and had to spend a few days in bed. He was visited by Nikolai Bukharin,

Lenin with Stalin at Gorki in 1922
Top: Trotsky going to his office at the Commissariat of War
Above right: Trotsky being filmed in the Kremlin

who told him: 'Lenin is very ill. He has had a stroke, and he cannot walk or talk. The doctors are utterly at a loss.' At that time, Trotsky writes, 'Bukharin was attached to me in his characteristic "Bukharin" way, half hysterically, half childishly. He finished his account of Lenin's illness by dropping down on my bed and muttering, as he pressed his arms about me over the blanket: "Don't you get sick, I implore you, don't get sick . . . There are two men of whose death I always think with horror – Lenin and you" . . . He was preventing me from concentrating on the alarm that his news had caused. The blow was overwhelming. It seemed as if the revolution itself were holding its breath.' Lenin convalesced in his country house at Gorki, a village near Moscow, where he gradually recovered: by October, he was back at work again in the Kremlin.

Early in December, a delegation from the union of educational workers came to Lenin and Trotsky with the request that Trotsky should take over the Commissariat of Education in addition to his other duties. 'Lenin wanted to know what I thought about it' [Trotsky writes]. 'I told him that in the educational field, as in every other, the difficulty would come from the administrative apparatus. "Yes, our bureaucratism is something monstrous," Lenin replied, picking up my train of thought. "I was appalled when I came back to

work . . . It is just because of this that you should not – or at least I think so – get drawn into any departmental work besides the military." Lenin proceeded to state his plan with passionate conviction. He had a limited amount of strength to give to the work of direction. He had three deputies. "You know them. Kamenev is, of course, a clever politician, but what sort of an administrator is he? Tsurupa is ill. Rykov is perhaps an administrator, but he will have to go back to the Supreme Economic Council. You must become a deputy. The situation is such that we must have a radical realignment of personnel." Again I pointed out the "apparatus" that made even my work in the war department increasingly difficult. "Well, that will be our chance to shake up the apparatus," Lenin retorted quickly, hinting at an expression I had once used. I replied that I referred to the bureaucracy not only in the state institutions, but in the party as well; that the cause of all the trouble lay in the combination of the two apparatuses and in the mutual shielding among the influential groups that gathered round the hierarchy of party secretaries. Lenin listened intently, and confirmed my suggestions in that deep tone which came straight from the chest, a tone that would break through in him only when, sure that the person he was talking to understood him completely, he would dispense with the conventionalities of conversation, and

October 1922 – Lenin, back in office after his illness, at the Council of People's Commissars. He is seated at the head of the table, with Rykov and Kamenov standing near him, and Trotsky seated fourth from the right. Right: Lenin convalescing at Gorki in 1922

touch openly on what was the most important and disturbing. After thinking it over for a moment, Lenin put the question pointblank: "You propose then to open fire not only against the state bureaucracy, but against the Organizational Bureau of the Central Committee as well?" I couldn't help laughing, this came so unexpectedly. "That seems to be it." The Organizational Bureau meant the very heart of Stalin's apparatus.

'"Oh, well," Lenin went on, obviously pleased that we had called the thing by its right name, "if that's the case, then I offer you a bloc against bureaucracy in general and against the Organizational Bureau in particular"...

'We agreed to meet again some time later. Lenin... planned to create a commission attached to the Central Committee for fighting bureaucracy. We were both to be members. The commission was essentially to be the

Trotsky engaged in administrative work at the Department for the Amelioration of Agriculture and Industry

lever for breaking up the Stalin faction as the backbone of the bureaucracy, and for creating such conditions in the party as would allow me to become Lenin's deputy, and, as he intended, his successor to the post of chairman of the Soviet of People's Commissars.' A few days after this conversation, Lenin suffered another stroke.

On 25 December, Lenin dictated his recommendations to the Central Committee of the Russian Communist Party which were later considered to embody his political testament:

'Our Party rests upon two classes, and for that reason its instability is possible, and if there cannot exist agreement between those classes its fall is inevitable. In such an event ... no measures would prove capable of preventing a split ... I think that the fundamental factor in the matter of stability – from this point of view – is such members of the central committee as Stalin and Trotsky. The relation between them constitutes, in my opinion, a big half of the danger of that split ... Comrade Stalin, having become general secretary, has concentrated enormous power in his hands; and I am not sure that he has always known how to use that power with sufficient caution. On the other hand Comrade Trotsky ... is distinguished not only by his exceptional abilities – personally he is, to be sure, the most able man in the present central committee – but also by his too far-reaching self-confidence and a disposition to be too much attracted by the purely administrative side of affairs. These two qualities of the two most able leaders of the present central committee might, quite innocently, lead to a split ...'

On 4 January 1923, Lenin added a postscript to

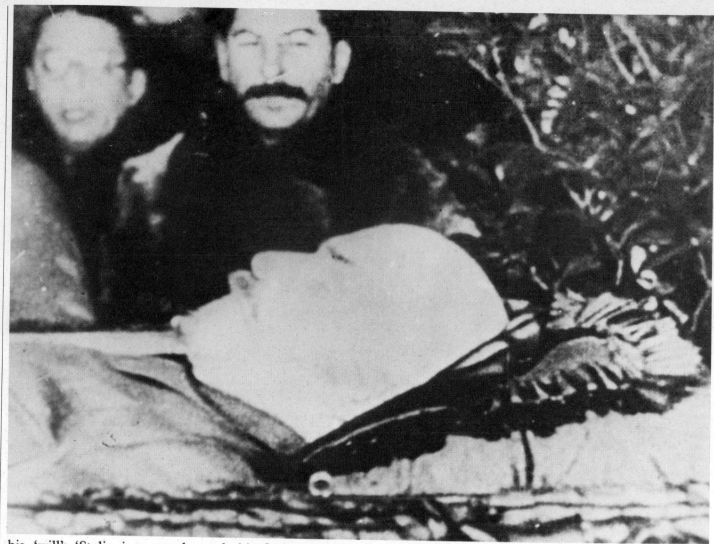

his 'will': 'Stalin is too rude, and this fault, entirely supportable in relations among us communists, becomes insupportable in the office of a general secretary. Therefore, I propose to the comrades to find a way to remove Stalin from the position and appoint to it another man who in all respects differs from Stalin in one superiority – namely, that he be more patient, more loyal, more polite and more considerate to comrades, less capricious, etc. This circumstance may seem an insignificant trifle, but I think that, from the point of view of preventing a split and from the point of view of the relation between Stalin and Trotsky which I discussed above, it is not a trifle, or it is such a trifle as may acquire a decisive significance.'

The return of Lenin's illness left the field clear for what Trotsky refers to as 'the conspiracy of the epigones'. Stalin, Zinoviev and Kamenev combined in a covert plot to undermine Trotsky's influence. They could not, at this stage, afford to make it public: Zinoviev and Kamenev had lost all moral authority in the party by their behaviour during 1917, and Stalin was still unknown to the people. They could only appeal openly to the prejudice against Trotsky of the 'old Bolsheviks', who had not forgiven his Menshevik past. The defeat of the revolutionary movement in Germany at the end of 1923 accelerated a shift to the right in the Bolshevik party. Throughout that year, during the 'interregnum' while Lenin was laid up at Gorki, the triumvirate worked secretly to form a cabal against Trotsky which could be concealed in the event of Lenin's recovery. 'These were hard days,' Natalya wrote in her memoirs, 'days of tense fighting for Lev Davydovich at the Politbureau against the rest of the members. He was alone and ill, and had to fight them all. Owing to his illness, the meetings were held in our apartment; I sat in the adjoining bedroom and heard his speeches. He spoke with his whole being; it seemed as if with every speech he lost some of his strength – he spoke with so much "blood". And in reply, I heard cold, indifferent answers. Everything, of course, had been decided in advance, so what was the need of getting excited? After each of these meetings, L.D.'s temperature mounted; he came out of his study soaked through, and undressed and went to bed. His linen and clothes had to be dried as if he had been drenched in a rainstorm. At that time, the meetings were frequent and were held in L.D.'s room, whose faded old carpet appeared in my dream every night in the shape of a live panther: the meetings during the day became nightmares. Such was the first stage of the struggle before it came out into the open.'

Trotsky had contracted a malarial infection in October; as his health continued to deteriorate under the strain, he had to be moved to the country. Early in 1924, his doctor insisted that he should leave for a cure at Sukhum, on the Black Sea. Trotsky and Natalya set off on the long train journey to the Caucasus. On the evening of 21 January, at the station in Tiflis, Trotsky was

Trotsky at Sukhum, 1924
Top: A. I. Mikoyan, V. M. Molotov and Stalin at Gorki during Lenin's lying-in-state
Above left: Stalin gazes enigmatically on the body of Lenin as it lies in state in Moscow

sitting in his carriage with a high temperature when his assistant handed him a telegram. It was from Stalin, and announced the news of Lenin's death. Trotsky telegraphed to the Kremlin: 'I deem it necessary to return to Moscow. When is the funeral?' In an hour he received the reply: 'The funeral will take place on Saturday, 26th. You will not be able to return on time. The Politbureau thinks that because of the state of your health you must proceed to Sukhum. Stalin.' In fact, the funeral took place on Sunday, 27th, and Trotsky could easily have attended it as the journey from Tiflis to Moscow took at the most four days. Still at the station, Trotsky jotted down a stunned tribute to the dead man, which was cabled to the Kremlin. 'Lenin is no more . . . These words fall upon our minds as heavily as a giant rock falls into the sea. Can one believe it? Can one make peace with this?' Then he travelled on to Sukhum.

'We arrived quite broken down', Natalya wrote. 'It was the first time we had seen Sukhum. The mimosa were in full bloom – they are plentiful there. Magnificent palms. Camellias . . . In the dining-room of the rest-house, there were two portraits on the wall, one – draped in black – of Vladimir Ilyich, the other of L.D. We felt like taking the latter one down, but thought it would look too demonstrative . . . Considerably delayed by the snow, the newspapers began to bring us the memorial speeches, obituaries and articles. Our friends were expecting L.D. to come to Moscow, and thought that he would cut short

Two pictures of Trotsky at Sukhum in March 1924. 'The attraction in hunting is that it acts on the mind as a poultice does on a sore'
Right: the fatal stay at Sukhum. Trotsky and Natalya, surrounded by aides, honour a local dignitary

his trip in order to return, since no one imagined that Stalin's telegram had cut off his return. I remember my son's letter, received at Sukhum. He was terribly shocked by Lenin's death, and though suffering from a cold, with a temperature of 104, he went in his not very warm coat to the Hall of Columns to pay his last respects, and waited, waited, and waited with impatience for our arrival. One could feel in his letter his bitter bewilderment and diffident reproach.'

The existence of Lenin's 'will' was known only to his secretary and to Krupskaya. After his death, she gave it to the secretariat of the central committee of the Russian Communist Party so that, as Lenin wished, it could be communicated to the next Party Congress. Zinoviev, Kamenev and Stalin planned to suppress the document, but Krupskaya insisted on its being made public. It was read by Kamenev to the central committee on the day before the opening session of the Thirteenth Congress in May. Trotsky, who had sufficiently recovered in health to return to Moscow in time for the congress, was present at the proceedings but kept silent throughout them. Zinoviev, on the other hand, had something to say. 'Comrades, the last wish of Ilyich, every word of Ilyich is without doubt law in our eyes. More than once we have vowed to fulfil everything which the dying Ilyich recommended us to do. You know well that we shall keep that promise . . . But we are happy to say that on one point Lenin's fears have not proved well founded. I mean the point about our general secretary.

You have all been witnesses of our work together in the last few months; and, like myself, you have been happy to confirm that Ilyich's fears have not been realized.' Against Krupskaya's wishes, it was decided not to read the testament at the congress, but to communicate it confidentially to the heads of the separate delegations attending the meetings. Any reference to it during the plenary sessions was banned, and it was forbidden to take notes during the private readings. None the less, its contents became known – and later Stalin was driven to denouncing it as a forgery. It was not until the end of 1927, when he had won his battle not only against Trotsky but against Zinoviev and Kamenev as well, that he felt able to admit its authenticity.

Trotsky's long absence from Moscow had fatally weakened his position as the most authoritative spokesman for the Opposition. Rykov had automatically succeeded Lenin as chairman of the Council of People's Commissars; and Rykov's position at the Supreme Economic Council had been filled by Felix Dzerzhinsky, the fanatical Pole who had been in control of the Cheka from its inception. E. M. Slyansky, Trotsky's deputy at the War Commissariat who had assumed his responsibilities there while he was away, had been summarily dismissed and replaced by Frunze – who, a year later, was to succeed Trotsky himself as War Commissar. The creation of a 'Lenin cult' was well advanced: every word of Lenin's was to be treated as Holy Writ, and phrases written during his various disputes with Trotsky could be used out of context to discredit the latter. This being the case, Trotsky showed almost inexplicable forbearance in refraining from any sort of protest against the partial suppression of Lenin's will.

For a year and a half, Trotsky had been levelling

criticisms at the government's policies. He had called for a return to socialist planning within the framework of the New Economic Policy, while most of the Bolsheviks had assumed the two concepts to be mutually exclusive. Accusing the Old Guard of 'bureaucratic degeneration', he had advocated a revival of proletarian democracy: to the Bolshevik dogma of a monolithic party rigidly disciplined by its party machine, he had opposed the idea of a party capable of absorbing many different shades of opinion, provided that they were compatible with its essential programme. Before his departure for Sukhum, he had been denounced as guilty of 'a petty bourgeois deviation from Leninism', and at the Thirteenth Congress he was treated as a heretic. Zinoviev spoke darkly of 'the growth of a new bourgeoisie' and 'the Indian summer of Menshevism', and demanded a recantation. Trotsky, in reply, denied that he had favoured factionalism, but blamed the party itself for inhibiting debate, thereby encouraging transient differences of thought to harden into factions. He refused to assent in his own condemnation, but stated that he would accept the party's decision even if he did not agree with it. 'The English have a historical proverb: "My country, right or wrong." With far greater historical right we can say: "Right or not right in individual particular concrete questions, but it is my party" . . .'

The State Publishers were in the process of bringing out a collected edition of Trotsky's *Works*, and the third volume, which consisted of his articles and speeches during 1917, was due for publication in October 1924. In September, Trotsky wrote a long preface to the book under the title *Lessons of October*. Here he reasserted his criticism of Lenin's formula of 'a democratic dictatorship of the peasantry and the proletariat': 'In certain circles in our party', he wrote, 'the emphasis in Lenin's formula was placed not on the *dictatorship* of the proletariat and the peasantry, but on its *democratic* character, which contrasted with a socialist character.' He pointed out that Lenin himself, in controversy with Kamenev in April 1917, had described the formula as outdated, and that from the moment of Trotsky's own return to Russia in May he had whole-heartedly supported Lenin's policy of the seizure of power by the proletariat. Kamenev was named as Lenin's principal opponent during the period from April to October, and both Zinoviev and Kamenev were reminded of their behaviour on the eve of the October insurrection itself. Stalin was not mentioned.

Lessons of October created an uproar: the triumvirate resorted to the use of any weapons in their counter-attack. Two years later, Kamenev admitted that 'the Trotskyite danger was invented for the purpose of our organized struggle against Trotsky.' At the time, he replied in a long, confused speech, which he delivered on three separate occasions, accusing Trotsky of 'under-estimating the peasantry' at Brest Litovsk, during the trade-unions debate, in his insistence on planning and in his criticism of the bureaucracy. Zinoviev published a hysterical article in both *Pravda* and *Izvestiya* called *Bolshevism or Trotskyism?*: 'The watchword of the day is

Trotsky in Red Square, before his resignation from the Army
Right: Trotsky with Christian Rakovsky
Top right: Trotsky with Red Army graduate officers in 1924

Bolshevization of all strata of the party! Ideological struggle against Trotskyism! Above all, enlightenment, enlightenment, enlightenment and once more enlightenment!' Stalin's intervention was more telling. He quoted two attacks on Lenin made by Trotsky in a hitherto unpublished letter written in 1913, and indicted three aspects of 'Trotskyism'. The theory of the permanent revolution, he said, ignored 'the poor peasantry as a revolutionary force'; Trotsky had no faith in the monolithic character of the Bolshevik party; and the 'new Trotskyism' was only a subtle variation on the old in its refusal to place Lenin on a pedestal.

Trotsky wrote a long and detailed reply to these and other slanders – but, mysteriously, decided not to publish it. His fever had returned, and once more his doctor advised him to go south. A meeting of the central com-

mittee held in January 1925 resulted in a long resolution which defined Trotskyism as 'a falsification of communism in the spirit of an approximation to "European" patterns of pseudo-marxism, i.e. in the last resort, in the spirit of "European" social-democracy'. It announced Trotsky's resignation from the position of President of the Revolutionary Military Council and People's Commissar for War, and the decision to launch a propaganda campaign in order to enlighten the masses as to the 'anti-Bolshevik character of Trotskyism'. Only two members of the central committee voted against the resolution: Christian Rakovsky and Yuri Pyatakov, both of whom had aligned themselves in Opposition with Trotsky in 1923. Rakovsky and Trotsky had been intimate friends since 1912, when Trotsky had been a war correspondent in the Balkans and Rakovsky had been the leader of the Rumanian Socialist party. Trotsky describes him, with affectionate admiration, in *My Life*: 'A Bulgarian by birth, Rakovsky . . . is a Rumanian subject by dint of the Balkan map, a French physician by education, a Russian by connections, by sympathies and by literary work . . . Rakovsky's personal traits, his broad international outlook, his profound nobility of character, have made him particularly odious to Stalin, who personifies the exact opposite of these qualities.'

After a second convalescence at Sukhum, where he spent three months, Trotsky returned to Moscow. In May 1925 he was appointed to serve on the Supreme Economic Council under Felix Dzerzhinsky. Dzerzhinsky (who died a year later) is described by Trotsky as 'a man of great and explosive passion . . . In every

discussion, even of things of minor importance, he would fire up, his nostrils would quiver, his eyes would sparkle, and his voice would be so strained that often it would break . . . Dzerzhinsky fell in love, in a mad infatuation, with everything he did, and guarded his associates from criticism and interference with a passionate fanaticism that had no element of the personal in it, for he was completely dissolved in his work. Dzerzhinsky had no opinions of his own. He never thought of himself as a politician, at least while Lenin was alive . . . In 1917 he joined the Bolsheviks . . . During the first two or three years, Dzerzhinsky was especially drawn to me. In his last years, he supported Stalin.'

Trotsky's new job entailed three separate chairmanships: of the Concessions Committee, the Board of Electrotechnical Development and the Industrial-Technological Commission. Engrossed in his new responsibilities, Trotsky worked hard for a rapid increase in industrialization and pioneered the development of the Dnieper Dam. Stalin, already exhibiting the complacent isolationism which he was soon to articulate in the doctrine of 'socialism in one country', remarked that the Dnieper power station was of no more use to Russia than a gramophone would be to a peasant without a cow. 'My practical work was performed under impossible conditions,' Trotsky writes. 'It is no exaggeration to say that much of the creative activity of Stalin and his assistant Molotov was devoted to organizing direct sabotage around me.'

Meanwhile, new alignments were forming in the party. 'In theoretical and political respects, both Zinoviev and Kamenev were probably superior to Stalin,' Trotsky continues. 'But they both lacked that little thing called character. Their international outlook, wider than

Trotsky, third from the right, on the Seventh Anniversary of the revolution
Left: Red Week, 1924 – left to right, Voroshilov, Trotsky, Kalinin, Frunze (with Budenny above him) and Clara Zetkin taking the salute on Lenin's mausoleum

The funeral of Felix Dzerzhinsky in 1926. Trotsky and Stalin are carrying the front of the coffin. Kalinin is in the foreground, Ry

on the left, and Kamenev's face can be seen between Trotsky and Stalin. This was Trotsky's last official appearance in Russia

Stalin's, which they acquired under Lenin in foreign exile, did not make their position any stronger; on the contrary, it weakened it. The political tendency was toward a self-contained national development . . . Zinoviev's and Kamenev's attempt to uphold the international viewpoint, if only to a limited degree, turned them into "Trotskyists" of the second order in the eyes of the bureaucracy. This led them to wage their campaign against me with even more fury, so that they might win greater confidence from the apparatus. But these efforts were also vain. The apparatus was rapidly discovering that Stalin was flesh of its flesh. Zinoviev and Kamenev soon found themselves in hostile opposition to Stalin; when they tried to transfer the dispute from the trio to the Central Committee, they discovered that Stalin had a solid majority there . . . To everyone's utter surprise, their own most of all, Zinoviev and Kamenev found themselves obliged to repeat word for word the criticisms by the Opposition, and soon they were listed as being in the camp of the "Trotskyists". It is little wonder that in our circle closer relations with Zinoviev and Kamenev seemed, to say the least, paradoxical . . . But such questions are finally decided not by psychological but by political considerations. Zinoviev and Kamenev openly avowed that the "Trotskyists" had been right in the struggle against them ever since 1923. They accepted the basic principles of our platform. In such circumstances, it was impossible not to form a bloc with them, especially since thousands of revolutionary Leningrad workers were behind them.'

A translation of *Where is Britain Going?*, which Trotsky had written at Sukhum in 1925, was published in England early the following year. In this book, he identified the two main revolutionary traditions in Britain with Cromwell and the Chartists, and argued that the British Communist Party, however weak, was the only legitimate inheritor of these. His attack on the Fabians and on the trade-union leaders caused considerable controversy. Most of his critics maintained that Trotsky, as a foreigner, had misunderstood the British Labour movement: but Bertrand Russell, writing in the *New Leader*, asserted that Trotsky was 'perfectly familiar with . . . [its] . . . political peculiarities'. However, Russell went on to deplore the fact that Trotsky appeared to be irresponsibly inciting the British people to a revolution, which might lead to an American blockade or a war that they would lose. Trotsky's reply sounds the same note that he had struck in his answer to Kautsky's denunciation of terrorism, and would strike again in his defence of Kronstadt: a sophisticated development of his natural bias towards reason, it may be described as a hyper-logical assault on the limits of logic. 'Revolutions are as a rule not made arbitrarily. If it were possible to map out the revolutionary road beforehand and in a rationalistic manner, then it would probably also be possible to avoid revolution altogether. Revolution is an expression of the impossibility of reconstructing class society by rationalist methods. Logical arguments, even if Russell turns them into mathematical formulae, are impotent against material

Dzerzhinsky's funeral procession. Trotsky is looking across the coffin at Stalin, both in white
Top: Trotsky at the funeral oration, separated from Stalin by a group including Zinoviev (standing next to Trotsky) and Voroshilov (at the microphone). Rykov is on Stalin's left

interests. The ruling classes will let civilization perish together with mathematics rather than give up their privileges . . .'

In May 1926, Trotsky and Natalya visited Berlin where he was induced to have his tonsils out: the operation, he remarks ironically, was a success – if one overlooks the fact that it was useless, as it did nothing to cure his recurrent fevers. While he was recovering in hospital, the German police informed him that they had foiled an

broken up. 'Zinoviev, after his usual vacillation, sided with me. Radek was opposed. Stalin clung to the bloc, even to the semblance of one, for all he was worth. The British trades unionists waited until their acute inner crisis was at an end, and then uncivilly kicked their generous but muddle-headed ally away.'

Trotsky's most impassioned criticism of the régime was directed against their policy in China. 'The Chinese Communist party was forced against its will to join the bourgeois Kuomintang party and submit to its military discipline. The creating of Soviets was forbidden. The Communists were advised to hold the agrarian revolution in check, and to abstain from arming the workers without the permission of the *bourgeoisie* . . . Since 1925, I had demanded the withdrawal of the Communists from the Kuomintang. The policy of Stalin and Bukharin not only prepared for and facilitated the crushing of the revolution but, with the help of reprisals by the state apparatus, shielded the counter-revolutionary work of Chiang Kai-Shek from our criticism. In April, 1927, at the party meeting in the Hall of Columns, Stalin still defended the policy of coalition with Chiang Kai-Shek and called for confidence in him. Five or six days later, Chiang Kai-Shek drowned the Shanghai workers and the Communist party in blood.' Confusion in the Comintern, caused by Stalin's concentration on his campaign against Trotsky, had allowed the Polish Communists to support Pilsudski; now, with the betrayal of the Chinese Communists, it was responsible for a greater set-back to the cause of world revolution.

Writing in his diary in 1935, Trotsky looked back upon this period: 'In 1926, when Zinoviev and Kamenev joined the Opposition after more than three years of plotting with Stalin against me, they gave me a number of not unnecessary warnings: "Do you think that Stalin is now considering how to reply to your arguments?" This was approximately what Kamenev said, in reference to my criticism of the Stalin-Bukharin-Molotov policies in China, England, etc. "You are mistaken. He is thinking of how to destroy you . . . To slander you, to trump up a military conspiracy, and then, when the ground has been prepared, to perpetrate a terroristic act. Stalin is conducting the war on a different plane from you. Your weapons are ineffective against him . . . As soon as we broke with Stalin, Zinoviev and I drew up something like a testament, in which we gave warning. that in the event of our 'accidental' death, Stalin should be considered responsible. This document is kept in a safe place. I advise you to do the same." Zinoviev told me, not without embarrassment, "Do you think that Stalin has not discussed the question of your physical removal? He has considered and discussed it thoroughly. He has always been held back by the same thought, that the young people would pin the responsibility on him personally, and would respond by acts of terrorism. He therefore believed that he first had to disperse the ranks of the oppositionist youth. But a job postponed is not a job abandoned. Take the necessary precautions."'

attempt on his life organized by the Russian White Guards. He was more disturbed, however, by news from Poland, where the Communist Party had supported Pilsudski in a petit-bourgeois rebellion which established him as dictator. Meanwhile, the prophecies made in *Where is Britain Going?* were partially – and prematurely – fulfilled by the General Strike. Trotsky excitedly followed its developments, but was appalled when the British trade-union leaders refused the aid which the Soviet trades unions had offered the strikers, and the British Communist Party refrained from condemning their caution. On Trotsky's return to Moscow, he indignantly insisted that the bloc between the Soviet trades unions and the General Council of the TUC should be

If the disaster in China appeared to strengthen the

Opposition (Trotsky wrote that 'we had grown more united intellectually, and stronger in numbers') it also strengthened Stalin's determination to crush it. The Oppositionist leaders prepared a statement of policy – their *Platform* – which they intended to place before the party at the Fifteenth Congress, to be held at the end of 1927. In September, the GPU raided the office where the *Platform* was printed, arrested several people working there, and announced that it had uncovered a conspiracy. It claimed that a former White Guard officer was involved in printing the *Platform*: in fact, such a figure did exist, but had been planted there by the GPU as an *agent provocateur*. Later that month, Trotsky was expelled from the executive of the Comintern. On 15 October he attended a session of the Central Soviet Executive in Leningrad with Zinoviev, who had recently been dismissed from the Chairmanship of the Leningrad Soviet. During a mass procession to honour the event, Trotsky and Zinoviev stood on a lorry some distance away from the official stands, deliberately isolated from the party leaders.

'The crowd had eyes only for them,' Victor Serge writes. 'After delivering hurrahs to order before Komarov, the new Chairman of the Soviet, the procession found itself level with these legendary men who no longer meant anything to the State. At this point the demonstrators made a silent gesture by lingering on the spot, and thousands of hands were outstretched, waving handkerchiefs or caps. It was a dumb acclamation, futile but still overwhelming. Zinoviev and Trotsky received the greeting in a spirit of happy determination, imagining

that they were witnessing a show of force. "The masses are with us!" they kept saying that night. Yet what possibilities were there in masses who were so submissive that they contained their emotions like this? As a matter of fact everybody in that crowd knew that the slightest gesture endangered his own and his family's livelihood.'

Encouraged by this episode, the Opposition organized a peaceful demonstration to coincide with the celebration of the Tenth Anniversary of the revolution on 7 November. Its members were to march in the official processions carrying banners with the following slogans:

Trotsky's sister Olga, the wife of L. B. Kamenev, working as head of the GPU in the Northern Caucasus
Top: a group of Oppositionists in Moscow, 1927 –
bottom row, left to right, Istchenko, I. Smirnov, Trotsky, I. Smilga, Alsky: Man Nevelson, the husband of Nina Bronstein, is second from the left in the top row

LA RUSSIE ILLUSTRÉE

ИЛЛЮСТРИРОВАННАЯ
РОССІЯ

Троцкій и троцкисты
Къ высылкѣ оппозиціи въ Сибирь

ПОСЛѢДНІЕ ДНИ
ВЪ МОСКВѢ...

A special issue, dealing with Trotsky and Trotskyism, of a
Russian émigré newspaper printed in Paris
Top: members of the Opposition on their way to exile in 1928
– seated left to right, L. Serebriakov, K. Radek, Trotsky,
M. Boguslavsky, E. Preobrazhensky; standing left to right,
C. Rakovsky, Y. Drobnis, A. Beloborodov, Seznovsky

'Down with the *kulak*, the NEP man and the bureaucrat!', 'Carry out Lenin's testament!', 'Speed up Industrialization!' and 'Preserve Bolshevik unity!' But Stalin
had had ample time to prepare. Anyone displaying an
Oppositionist banner was attacked by the police, and
when Trotsky himself tried to speak in Red Square there
were shouts of 'Down with Trotsky, the Jew, the traitor!'
and a policeman shot at his car, shattering the windscreen.
That evening, Trotsky quietly left his lodgings at the
Kremlin for a small room in a friend's house. It is ironic
that the Tenth Anniversary celebrations had been intended to include the showing of Sergei M. Eisenstein's
new film, *October*. At the last moment, it was discovered
that Trotsky was portrayed in it as the hero and central
figure of the insurrection. Profoundly embarrassed, the
organizers hastily cancelled the performance and
Eisenstein was ordered to re-edit his work. When it was
eventually shown in March 1928, those members of the
audience who had lived through the events depicted on
the screen could recognize all the salient elements –
except for Trotsky, whose role had been so minimized
that it had become totally distorted.

On 14 November 1927, the anathema was form-
alized: Trotsky and Zinoviev were expelled from the
party, and Rakovsky, Kamenev and I. Smilga (an 'old
Bolshevik' who had joined the Opposition) were expelled
from the Central Committee. Two days later, Zinoviev,
Kamenev and Karl Radek were unceremoniously evicted
from the Kremlin. Victor Serge describes Radek that
evening 'in the process of sorting and destroying his

papers, which were scattered in the middle of a deluge of old books heaped in confusion over the carpets. "I'm selling all this for buttons", he told me, "and then I'm clearing out. We've been absolute idiots! We haven't a halfpenny, when we could have kept back some pretty spoils of war for ourselves! Today we are being killed off through lack of money. We with our celebrated revolutionary honesty, we've just been over-scrupulous sods of intellectuals." Then, without a pause, as though it were about the most commonplace matter: "Yoffe killed himself tonight. He left a political testament addressed to Leon Davidovich, which the GPU of course stole in a flash. But I got there in time, and I've fixed a nice scandal for them abroad if they don't give it back.'"

Adolf Abramovich Yoffe had shot himself in the Kremlin. He had recently returned from Japan, where he had been the Soviet Ambassador, to work as Trotsky's deputy on the Concessions Committee. He was seriously ill with tuberculosis, but Stalin had forbidden him to travel abroad for a cure. The long letter he had left

doubted the rightness of the road you pointed out, and as you know I have gone with you for more than twenty years, since the days of "permanent revolution". But I have always believed that you lacked Lenin's *unbending will*, his *unwillingness to yield*, his readiness even to remain alone on the path that he thought right in the anticipation of a future majority, of a future recognition by everyone of the rightness of his path. *Politically, you were always right*, beginning with 1905, and I told you repeatedly that with my own ears I had heard Lenin admit that even in 1905, *you, and not he*, were right. One does not lie before his death, and now I repeat this again to you .. But you have often *abandoned your rightness* for the sake of an overvalued agreement, or compromise. This is a mistake. I repeat: politically you have always been right, but now *more right than ever*. Some day the party will realize it, and history will not fail to accord recognition. Then don't lose your courage if someone leaves you now, or if not as many come to you, and not as soon, as we all would like. You are right, but the guarantee of the victory of your rightness lies in nothing but the extreme unwillingness to yield, the strictest straightforwardness, the absolute rejection of all compromise: in this very thing lay the secret of Lenin's victories. Many a time I have wanted to tell you this, but only now have I brought myself to do so, as a last farewell.'

Trotsky took these words to heart: the end of his life was an exalted but often painful exercise in the rejection of compromise and the preservation, at whatever cost, of integrity between action and belief. Yoffe's funeral was arranged to take place on a working day, in order to discourage crowds – but thousands of people followed the coffin through the streets. Trotsky, Rakovsky and Ivan Smirnov were the chief mourners, and Trotsky made a speech by the grave. This was to be his last public appearance in Russia. The Joint Opposition was rapidly

Trotsky speaking at Yoffe's funeral on 19 November 1927 – his last public speech in Russia
Above left: Trotsky with Adolph Yoffe

behind was eventually handed over to Rakovsky, who restored it to Trotsky. It told the tragic story of a life dedicated so whole-heartedly to the noble cause of socialism that it could no longer sustain the disillusion caused by recent developments in Russia. Part of it was addressed directly to Trotsky:

'You and I, dear Lev Davidovich, are bound to each other by decades of joint work, and, I make bold to hope, of personal friendship. This gives me the right to tell you in parting what I think you are mistaken in. I have never

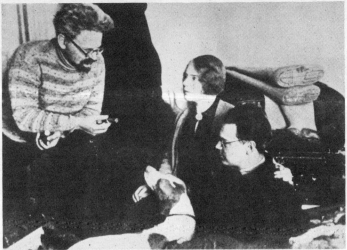

Trotsky, Natalya and Leon Sedov (Lyova) in exile at Alma Ata
Left: Trotsky in the snow at Alma Ata, 1928

disintegrating. 'The only concern of Zinoviev and his friends was to capitulate while there was still time,' Trotsky writes. 'They hoped to buy forgiveness, if not to win favour, by a demonstrative break with me at the time of the Fifteenth Congress. They did not foresee that by a double betrayal they would achieve their own political elimination.' On 18 December, Zinoviev and Kamenev recanted; Bukharin is said to have received them with the ominous words: 'You have done well to make up your mind – this was the last minute – the iron curtain of history is about to come down.' They were shortly followed by Yuri Pyatakov, Nikolai Krestinsky, Vladimir Antonov-Ovseenko, and more than 3,300 adherents of the Opposition. For Trotsky, and those other members of the Left Opposition who refused to recant, retribution came swiftly from the GPU in the form of banishment.

Trotsky, Natalya and their elder son Lyova left Moscow in January, 1928 for exile in Central Asia. 'We spent a year at Alma Ata,' Natalya writes, 'a town of earthquakes and floods, at the foot of the Tyan-Shan range on the borders of China 250 kilometres from the railway and 4,000 from Moscow, a year spent with letters, books and nature.' Although Natalya took pleasure in the snow – 'white, clean and dry' – and the bright red poppies that emerged in the spring, it was a dismal year for the family. Trotsky suffered a recurrence of his old malarial infection. In June, he heard from Rakovsky that his daughter Nina had died; her sister Zina was too ill to join him at Alma Ata. His younger son Sergei, less political than Lyova, was at Moscow, while Alexandra remained in isolation at Leningrad, a centre for the few Trotskyist supporters who remained there. On the Eleventh Anniversary of the revolution, it became clear that Stalin had done a neat about face and adopted the very policies which had been condemned as Trotskyist heresies a year before. The same slogans attacking the *kulak*, the NEP man and the bureaucrat, while calling for the speed-up of industrialization, became the official *dicta* on which his new platform was based. Now that Stalin had stolen the thunder of the Left Opposition, he came in for criticism from Bukharin, Rykov, Michail Tomsky and others to the right of the party. For a moment, it even seemed

anished from Russia, Trotsky and Natalya arrive at Constantinople in January 1929, and are taken at once to the Soviet Consulate

possible that a bloc against Stalin might be formed between Trotsky and the Bukharinists: this never took place, but the fact that he did not immediately reject the idea lost Trotsky some sympathy from Radek, Preobrazhensky, Smilga, Serebriakov and Smirna, Oppositionists who would have preferred to form a coalition with Stalin and the centre than with Bukharin and the right. Stalin now needed support from the left; and Trotsky's continued presence, even in Alma Ata, was an impediment to his getting it.

In October, the censorship had started to restrict Trotsky's correspondence. After he had protested in December against this postal blockade, he was visited by a GPU official and presented with an ultimatum: if he did not cease his 'counter-revolutionary activity' he would be completely isolated from politics and forced to change his place of residence. Trotsky replied in a letter to the International: 'To demand from me that I renounce my political activity is to demand that I abjure the struggle which I have been conducting in the interests of the international working-class, a struggle in which I have been ceaselessly engaged for thirty-two years, during the whole of my conscious life . . . Only a bureaucracy corrupt to its roots can demand such a renunciation . . .' The defiant challenge was answered within a month: on 20 January 1929, the GPU official served Trotsky with a deportation order banishing him 'from the entire territory of the U.S.S.R.'.

At dawn two days later the family, under escort, set off on a strange journey by car and sleigh over the dangerous snowdrifts through freezing wind and storm. At last they reached a train. When the news reached him that he was being deported to Constantinople, Trotsky refused to travel further: 'Our train, turned aside from the direction in which it has been going, moves along slowly, stops on a side-line near a dead little station, and there sinks into a coma between two stretches of thin woods. Day after day goes by. The number of empty cans about the train grows steadily. Crows and magpies gather for the feast in ever-increasing flocks. Waste . . . Solitude . . . There are no hares here; they were wiped out in the autumn by a cruel epidemic, and so the fox has laid his stealthy tracks to the very train. The engine makes daily trips with one car to a larger station for our midday meal and our newspapers. Grippe rages in our car. We reread Anatole France . . . Our engine keeps rolling back and forth over the rails to keep from freezing. In the ether, radio stations call to one another, asking our whereabouts. We don't hear these inquiries; we are playing chess. But even if we heard them, we could not answer; we were brought here at night, and we ourselves don't know where we are. Thus we spent twelve days and twelve nights. We learned from the newspapers of new arrests of several hundred people, including 150 of the so-called "Trotskyist centre".' Orders came from Moscow that the deportation must be enforced, and the train resumed its journey. 'The steamer Kalinin had been appointed to take us from Odessa, but it became icebound and all the efforts of the ice-breakers were in vain. Moscow was standing on the telegraph line and urging haste. The steamer Ilyich put on steam by urgent order. Our train arrived at Odessa on the night of 10 February. I looked through the car window at familiar places; I had spent seven years of my school life in this city . . . After a journey of twenty-two days, during which we had covered a distance of 6,000 kilometres, we found ourselves in Constantinople.'

118 | **Kalinin's birthday party, 1929: left to right, Molotov, Mikoyan, Stalin, Kamenev, Voroshilov, Kalinin and Budenny celebrate**

Exile 1929-1940

Trotsky aged fifty-seven — 'mug-shots' taken by the police when he was granted asylum in Mexico

The first four years of Trotsky's third and final foreign exile were spent on one of the Prinkipo Islands in a large but dilapidated villa rented from a bankrupt Turkish Pasha. This remote retreat, to which royal rivals of the Byzantine Emperors had once been banished, could only be reached by steamer from Constantinople, an hour and a half's journey away. Trotsky described Büyük Ada, his new home, as a 'red-cliffed island set in deep blue' which seemed to crouch in the

Sea of Marmara 'like a prehistoric animal drinking'. Here he could indulge his passion for fishing, that 'diverter of sadness and calmer of unquiet thoughts'. He became particularly attached to a young Greek fisherman, Kharalambos, who was almost illiterate but 'could read like an artist the beautiful book of Marmara'. The last chapter of Trotsky's autobiography, written at Prinkipo, has a haunting title – 'The Planet Without A Visa'. Entry permits were denied to him successively

by Germany, Great Britain, France, Czechoslovakia, the Netherlands, Austria, Norway, and even by Luxemburg. Officialdom everywhere, it seemed, either hated Trotsky or feared him, despite his apparently powerless position. Winston Churchill, in an essay called 'The Ogre of Europe', openly gloated over the man whose frown had once 'meted death to thousands' and who now sat disconsolate, 'a bundle of old rags, stranded on the shores of the Black Sea'. Trotsky – a most improbable contributor to the Beaverbrook Press – wrote a series of articles in the *Daily Express* giving his reasons for wishing to live in England; but Ramsay Macdonald and his Labour Ministers were as determined as Churchill that the 'ogre' should remain stranded. It took George Bernard Shaw to

point out the irony of a socialist government 'refusing the right of asylum to a very distinguished Socialist while granting it to the most reactionary opponents' and the absurdity of assuming that Trotsky could be silenced by excluding him from Britain. 'His trenchant literary power, and the hold which his extraordinary career has given him on the public imagination of the modern world, enable him to use every attempt to persecute him . . . He becomes the inspirer and the hero of all the militants of the extreme left of every country.'

As a place of asylum, Turkey had two main disadvantages from Trotsky's point of view. He felt himself cut off from the rest of the world there, and at the same time disconcertingly vulnerable to retaliation from the

Trotsky (left) with Natalya and Sobolevicius-Senin on a
sailing excursion at Prinkipo. Years later, Natalya defaced the
image of Senin with red ink and added *Provocateur*

The *Evening Standard* reproduces *Pravda*'s reaction to
Trotsky's first article in the *Daily Express*

GPU and the White émigrés. The house was surrounded
by sentries drawn from the Turkish police, and filled with
secretaries doing double duty as personal bodyguards:
but these, however zealous, could not prevent the pene-
tration into his household of *agents provocateurs*. A
Russian called Valentine Olberg persistently offered his
services as a secretary, but friends in Berlin warned
Trotsky in time that Olberg was an informer. No warning
was received, however, against a Latvian named Franck
who stayed for five months at Prinkipo and was later discovered to be a spy for the GPU. A certain Sobolevicius,

alias Senin, was also a visitor to Büyük Ada; at the time
Trotsky had complete confidence both in him and his
brother, Dr Soblen, alias Roman Well. Thirty years later,
when Sobolevicius, now known as Jack Soble, was
arrested in the U.S.A. as a Soviet agent, he confessed that
he had spied on Trotsky at Prinkipo. The pattern thus
created at the start of his exile – bored, inefficient guards
provided by the local police on the outside; devoted young
secretaries prepared to risk their lives in his defence on
the inside; and everywhere the constant menace of the
agent provocateur – was to repeat itself until the very end.
At the centre of this uneasy circle, he never abandoned
his self-appointed task, and continued to analyse, to
prophesy and to accuse.

In July 1929 Trotsky issued the first number of the
Russian *Bulletin of the Opposition*, first published in Paris,
then in Berlin, Paris and the U.S.A. This was the official
organ of the International Left Opposition (Bolshevik-
Leninist) which was dedicated to recalling the Third
Communist International to Leninist principles and
practice. The *Bulletin* was an important platform for
Trotsky, through which he could maintain contact with
the Left Opposition in Russia. He completed *The Permanent Revolution*, which he had begun at Alma Ata, and
gathered together a collection of documents which the
Soviet Union had suppressed in a volume called *The Stalin
School of Falsification*. During the next three years he
wrote copiously on the 'problems' of both the Spanish and
the Chinese revolutions, and on Hitler's rise to power –
which he foretold as early as September 1930.

In addition to these polemical and theoretical
writings, Trotsky also produced two undisputed literary
masterpieces while he was living at Prinkipo. *My Life* has

125

Trotsky jubilant after catching a snoek

Natalya soon after her arrival at Prinkipo

Trotsky with his fisherman friend, Kharalambos

Trotsky wearing deep-sea fisherman's harness on the waters of the Sea of Marmara

Visitors to Prinkipo: left to right, Pierre Naville, Trotsky, Gérard Rosenthal, Mme Naville. Naville had been expelled from the Communist Party in 1927 because of his Trotskyist sympathies. Rosenthal was Trotsky's lawyer in France

Trotsky's study at Büyük Ada. It was at this desk that he wrote *My Life* and his classic *History of the Russian Revolution*

The villa at Büyük Ada, Trotsky's home from 1929–33

Left: Trotsky's cook displays an eel he had caught.
Right: Jean van Heijenoort, Trotsky's secretary from 1932

AN UNDESIRABLE.

HOME SECRETARY. "WE CAN'T HAVE YOU HERE."
TROTSKY. "BUT I'M AN OLD FRIEND OF THE HOUSE."
HOME SECRETARY. "YES, I KNOW. THAT'S WHY."

[During an interview in which he gave various reasons for his request to be permitted to visit England, TROTSKY is reported to have said : "The party which for the second time assumes power in Great Britain believes that the difficulties created by private ownership can be surmounted. . . . I want to see how it will be done." Mr. Punch's cartoon expresses a speculative hope, not a prediction, that TROTSKY's curiosity will be discouraged.]

Punch reacted predictably to Trotsky's application for a British visa in 1929, but G. B. Shaw advised those 'who had an unreasoning dread of him as a caged lion' to admit him to Britain 'if only to hold the key of his cage'

been acknowledged as one of the world's greatest autobiographies: it reveals a much more 'human' Trotsky than is shown by his purely political writings, and in it his intellectual distinction is tempered by both a sense of beauty and a sense of fun. While he was still correcting the French and German translations of *My Life*, he was already preparing the synopsis of his three-volume *History of the Russian Revolution*. Many tributes have been paid to this monumental work: one of the most interesting comes from a slightly unexpected quarter, the historian A. L. Rowse, who could hardly be described as a Marxist critic. In *End of an Epoch*, Rowse wrote:

'The real importance of Trotsky's *History* does not lie in his power of word painting, either of character or of scene, though indeed his gift is so brilliant and incisive that one is continually reminded of Carlyle. There is something of the same technique, the same mannerism even, in the way the rapid lights shift across the scene and particular odd episodes are brought out in singular sharpness of relief and made to bear general significance; something of the same difficulty in following the sequel of events – the lights are so blinding – one may add. But where Carlyle had but his magnificent powers of intuition to rely on, Trotsky has a theory of history at his command, which enables him to grasp what is significant and to relate things together. The same point can be illustrated more appositely by comparison with Winston Churchill's *The World Crisis*, for the two men are not dissimilar in character and gifts of mind. But here again one notices the difference; for Mr Churchill's history, for all its personality, its vividness, and vitality, points which it has in common with Trotsky – has not a philosophy of history behind it.'

At the end of 1932, the 'lion' was briefly let out of his cage when Danish Social Democratic students invited Trotsky to lecture at Copenhagen 'in defence of the October Revolution' on its Fifteenth Anniversary. Travelling as Mr Sedov, he left Constantinople on 14 November with Natalya and three secretaries: Jan Fraenkel, Pierre Frank and Oscar Cohn. The journey received an embarrassing amount of publicity: Europe was still afraid of Trotsky, and fascinated by the object of its fear. At Naples he was given only one hour in which to visit the ruins of Pompeii, accompanied by a heavy police escort, and he was not allowed to get off at Athens at all. Forbidden to disembark at Marseilles, he was transferred at sea to a motor-boat which deposited him at a remote landing-stage outside the town. From here he was rushed across France by car, with reporters in pursuit, while the right-wing press denounced him as 'the traitor of Brest Litovsk'. When he arrived at Copenhagen on 23 November, he was met with hostility from both the Danish Royal Family, who were related to the Tsar's family, and the local communists, who were loyal to Stalin. He first stayed in a rented villa which had belonged to a popular dancer and was prettily decorated in an ultra-feminine and rather anachronistic style, but after the press had discovered his whereabouts he moved to a

The unwelcome visitor 'rushed across France by car'
Left: Trotsky outside Marseilles on his way to Denmark in 1932
Overleaf: Trotsky's speech at Copenhagen

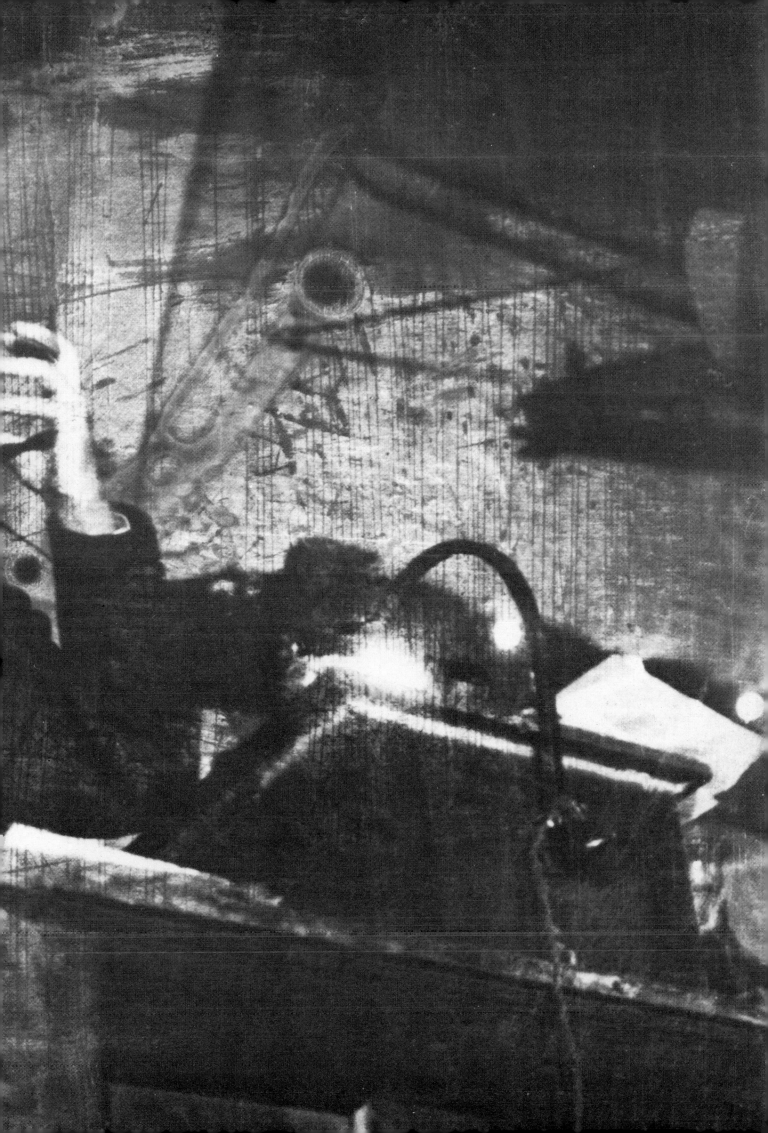

The broadcast for CBS at Copenhagen

those who heard it, he broadcast in English for CBS – the Danish radio having refused him air-time. He pointed out to his American listeners that valid criticism of recent developments in the Soviet Union should stop short of condemning the October Revolution itself; the American Civil War had shocked contemporaries, yet it had led to the United States of the present day 'with its unbounded practical initiative, its rationalized technology, its economic *élan*'. He also told French reporters that he would never deny his collaboration to Stalin, should it be required; politics, he insisted, was concerned with neither personal rivalry nor the spirit of revenge.

Trotsky's Danish visa expired after eight days. The party travelled by boat to Antwerp, and by train to Paris, where police at the station cordoned them off from the crowd. Lyova, who was living in Berlin, was waiting at the Gare du Nord; Edouard Herriot had granted Natalya's request that he should be allowed to join them on the journey to Marseilles. No boat to Constantinople was due for nine days, and they hoped for a little longer time with their son; but the French government were so anxious to be rid of their unwelcome visitor that he was hurriedly put on the first train leaving the country, which happened to be going to Venice. By 12 December, he was back at Prinkipo.

After Hitler became Chancellor in January 1933, Trotsky wrote in the *Bulletin* that a failure of the German Communist Party 'to form a united front and to set up

suburban boarding-house. It was rumoured that his various enemies were planning to disrupt the lecture, and he was surrounded by a double guard of Danish police and his own followers. The latter included Pierre Naville and Raymond Molinier, who headed rival Trotskyist groups in Paris; his German lawyer, who had been Karl Liebknecht's associate; and Gérard Rosenthal, his lawyer in France. Rosenthal concealed himself beneath a table on the platform, clutching a gun, while Trotsky spoke in German for two hours to an audience of two thousand people. In addition to the lecture, which passed off without disturbance and made a lasting impression on

Trotsky alighting at the Gare du Nord on 6 December 1932, with his secretary, Jan Fraenkel

Jean van Heijenoort and Max Schachtman after receiving Trotsky's French visa from the consul at Constantinople in July 1933
Right: at St Palais, Royan, 1933 – left to right, Rudolf Klement, Trotsky, Yvan Craipeau (a visiting Trotskyist), Jeanne Martin (Lyova's second wife), Sara Weber; in the front, Jean van Heijenoort

local defence committees, which might become Soviets tomorrow, will be nothing less than a surrender to fascism . . . Should such a disaster happen, the working class will have to make its way towards a Fourth International; and it will have to make it through mountains of corpses and years of unbearable sufferings and calamities.' In March, the German Communist Party capitulated to the Nazis without firing a shot, and its policy was approved by the Third Communist International. Trotsky saw this collapse as an ignominious repetition of the débâcle of the Second International in August 1914, when Lenin, Rosa Luxemburg, Karl Liebknecht and Trotsky himself had proclaimed the need for the Third International. He now finally renounced all allegiance to the Third International – a decisive move, but a bitter one for him to make. In July, the small and isolated International Left Opposition transformed itself into the International Communist League (Bolshevik-Leninist) and the idea of the Fourth International was formally proposed. But the going was slow: a conference held three years later in Europe did not succeed in establishing the Fourth International, in spite of Trotsky's urging, and it was not until 1938 that the World Party of Socialist Revolution was founded. Even then, a few Trotskyists feared that the ceremony might be seen as an empty gesture which would do the cause more harm than good.

Trotsky had been expelled for ever from France in 1916; but his supporters there had renewed the campaign to get him a residence permit, and in July 1933 the new Daladier government granted him a visa. This was conditional on his remaining in the south, never visiting Paris at all, keeping strictly incognito and submitting to police surveillance. He left Turkey on an Italian boat, accompanied by Natalya, Max Shachtman – an American Trotskyist who had been expelled from the Communist Party in 1928 – and three secretaries: Jean van Heijenoort, Rudolf Klement and Sara Weber. On 24 July, the ship was stopped out at sea before reaching Marseilles, where a crowd of reporters were awaiting Trotsky's arrival, and a small tugboat, containing Lyova and Raymond Molinier, transported him to Cassis instead: here he was solemnly handed a document revoking the original expulsion order. As in the previous year, right-wing newspapers were loudly protesting against his admission, and both GPU agents and journalists were desperately trying to pick up his trail. A villa had been rented for the party at St Palais, near Royan, on the Atlantic coast. Here Trotsky remained until 1 October, spending most of the time in bed: he had become painfully ill with lumbago during the voyage. His incognito had been so successfully preserved that the Stalinists, in spite of their efforts, had failed to discover his whereabouts; the government therefore relaxed their embargo on his moving away from the south. On 1 October, slightly better in health, he went with Natalya for a rest-cure in the Pyrenees, during which he paid a disgusted visit to Lourdes; and a month later they settled

into another house, outside Barbizon, on the edge of the forest of Fontainebleau, hidden in a small park and guarded by sentries and watchdogs.

The secret of Trotsky's new address was kept for six months – and then it only leaked out after Rudolf Klement had been stopped by the local police for some trivial driving offence. Immediately, the right-wing press renewed its uproar. The Ministry of the Interior, embarrassed, served an expulsion order on Trotsky but did not enforce it as no other country would receive him. He was advised, however, to leave Barbizon. While van Heijenoort distracted the crowds that had gathered in front of the house, Trotsky escaped by a back door on the evening of 15 April 1934. He spent a few days in Paris with Lyova, and then drove southwards, accompanied by van Heijenoort and Molinier, moving aimlessly from one hotel to another. 'An agent of the *Sûreté générale* followed close on our heels,' he wrote in his diary a year later. 'We stopped at Chamonix . . . Early in the morning, in a barbershop, M[olinier] read in a local newspaper a sensational notice about our whereabouts. N[atalya] had just arrived from Paris to join me. We managed to disappear before the notice could create the necessary effect. We had a small, rather antique Ford: its description and registration number appeared in print. We had to get rid of that car and buy another, also a Ford, but a still older model . . . We decided to rent a summer place in some spot away from the frontier . . . [and to] . . . put up in a *pension* while the search went on. But this did not prove to be so simple: we could not register with our own documents, and the police would not allow us to register with false ones. Actually, French citizens are not required to show their documents; but in a *pension* with a *table d'hôte* we would have some trouble passing for French . . . We decided to be French citizens of foreign extraction. To this end we enlisted the services of a young French comrade with a Dutch name (van Heijenoort) to play the part of our nephew. How to get rid of the *table d'hôte*? I proposed that we should don mourning and give this as an excuse for eating in our own room. The "nephew" was to eat at the common table and observe the goings-on in the house.

'The plan encountered, first of all, resistance from N[atalya]: to put on mourning and engage in dissimulation – she regarded this as something offensive to her very self. But the advantages of the plan were obvious, and she had to give in. Our arrival at the *pension* could not have gone better. Even the three South American students living there – a breed little inclined to discipline – stopped talking and bowed respectfully to people in mourning. I was only a little surprised at the engravings hanging in the hall: "The King's Cavalryman", "The Parting of Marie Antoinette with her Children", and the like. The riddle was quickly solved. After dinner our "nephew" came to us very much disturbed: we had landed in a royalist *pension*! . . .

'Just at the time of our stay in the *pension* the weekly *L'Illustration* printed a large photograph of both N[atalya]

134 | **Right: Trotsky with his guard dogs Benno and Stella at Royan**

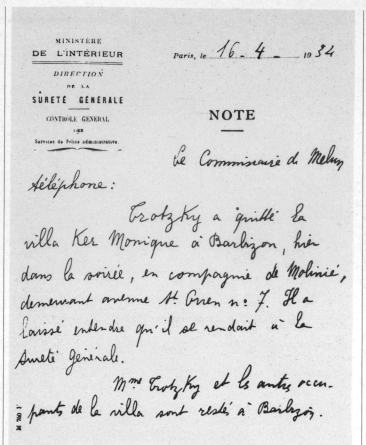

MINISTÈRE
DE L'INTÉRIEUR

DIRECTION
DE LA
SÛRETÉ GÉNÉRALE

CONTRÔLE GÉNÉRAL
1=88
Services de Police administrative.

Paris, le 16-4- 1934

NOTE

Le Commissaire de Melun
téléphone :

Trotzky a quitté la villa Ker Monique à Barbizon, hier dans la soirée, en compagnie de Molinié, demeurant avenue St. Ouen n° 7. Il a laissé entendre qu'il se rendait à la Sûreté Générale.

Mme Trotzky et les autres occupants de la villa sont restés à Barbizon.

A note from the Ministry of the Interior to the Sûreté Générale announcing Trotsky's arrival in Paris

Jean van Heijenoort (alias M. Marcel) pacifies the press on the day after Trotsky's escape from Barbizon

The Villa Ker Monique at Barbizon

Crowds at Barbizon trying to catch a glimpse of Trotsky

and me. I was not easily recognizable with my moustache and beard shaved off and my haircut changed, but N[atalya]'s likeness was very good . . . But we were firm, and remained within the royalist roof until we had rented a summer house.'

They found a suitable cottage, but here again Trotsky had bad luck: when the Prefect of the Department learnt their new address, he was appalled. 'You have chosen a most inappropriate place! That is a hotbed of clericalism. The mayor is a personal enemy of mine!' Sure enough, all the walls in the house were hung with crucifixes and pious engravings. Trotsky at first refused to budge; but when the Prefect began to hint at his whereabouts to the local press, he had to move on in a hurry. At last, he and Natalya came to rest at Domesne, near Grenoble, in June 1934. Armed with false papers in the names of Level Léon Louis and his wife Anna Natalie, they stayed with the village teacher and lived in complete isolation, without any entourage, for nearly a year.

Trotsky compared his life at Domesne to confinement in a moderately comfortable prison. It was a lonely and melancholy time for him. Since his arrival in France, all his links with the Opposition in the Soviet Union had been broken: one by one, its leaders had capitulated to Stalin, and their subsequent recantations had become ever wilder and more abject. For a while he had been sustained by trust in the loyalty of Christian Rakovsky, whom he loved as a 'friend, fighter and thinker'; but in

The front of Trotsky's false identification papers at Grenoble

Form fields (left):

Valable pour les années 19.., 19..
ou jusqu'au (1) ....

Délivrée par M. le Préfet de _l'Isère_
le _7 juin 1934_
en remplacement de la Carte N° ....
délivrée le ....
Pièces d'identité fournies : ....

Je certifie exactes les déclarations ci-contre.
(Signature de l'étranger)

Date de la demande de carte _24 mai 1934_

Case réservée au Service central.

(1) Date d'expiration de la validité du visa pour les étrangers titulaires de visa à durée limitée.

Form fields (right):

Nom : _Lanis_
Prénoms : _Kevel Léon_
né le _1 mai 1879_
à _Bucarest_
fil... de ....
né le .... à ....
et de ....
née le .... à ....
Profession : _Professeur honoraire_
Nationalité : _Roumaine_
Mode d'acquisition de cette nationalité : filiation, ~~mariage, naturalisation~~. (Rayer les mentions inutiles.)
Situation de famille : ~~célibataire~~, marié, ~~veuf~~, ~~divorcé~~. (Rayer les mentions inutiles.)
Adresse : Localité : _Grenoble_ / Rue et N° : _Hôtel Moderne_
Renseignements sur le conjoint : Nom : _Lanis née Vitis_ / Prénoms : _Anna Natalie_ / Née le _24 9bre 1882 à Kichinev_ / Nationalité d'origine : _Roumaine_

Enfants au-dessous de 15 ans.

PRÉNOMS	AGE	LIEU DE NAISSANCE	OBSERVATIONS

The back, giving his assumed name and nationality

February, while Trotsky was still at Barbizon, the bitter news had reached him that Rakovsky had defected too. 'One great revolutionary less, one petty official more!' he wrote in his diary. 'Rakovsky was virtually my last contact with the old revolutionary generation. After his capitulation there is nobody left . . . For a long time now I have not been able to satisfy my need to exchange ideas and discuss problems with someone else. I am reduced to carrying on a dialogue with the newspapers . . .'

It was over his wireless set in Grenoble that Trotsky heard the details of the 'Kirov affair'; grimly and intently, he analysed its implications. Sergei Kirov, who had replaced Zinoviev in the Politbureau nine years before, was assassinated on 1 December 1934, by a young man called Nikolayev. At first a conspiracy of White Guards was held responsible, but then the blame dramatically shifted direction and Trotsky, Zinoviev and Kamenev were accused of inspiring the deed. The assassin and fourteen others were executed; thousands of people, suspected of supporting Trotsky or Zinoviev, were deported to concentration camps; Zinoviev was sentenced to ten years in prison, and Kamenev to five. Trotsky, convinced that the GPU had known of the murder in advance and had condoned it, now feared that Stalin would do a deal with Zinoviev and Kamenev, offering to rehabilitate them if they would denounce Trotsky as the leader of a terrorist organization. He also realized that the incident had started a chain of events which would

Zinaida Volkov (Zina) at Prinkipo, 1931

increase the danger not only to himself, but to his whole family as well: his younger son, his first wife, his two sons-in-law and all but one of his grandchildren were still in the Soviet Union and hideously vulnerable.

Leon Sedov, Trotsky's elder son, had accompanied his parents to Prinkipo, leaving his wife and child in Moscow. Lyova shared his father's absorbing passion for politics, and during his exile became his right-hand man. Their relationship is described by Isaac Deutscher in *The Prophet Outcast:* 'They were in full political concord, and Lyova's adoration for his father amounted to identification. Yet it was this identification that was also a cause of strain. Trotsky had an uneasy feeling that his own personality and interests had imposed themselves too overwhelmingly on Lyova, and that he had reduced Lyova to the frustrating part of the great man's little son. Yet he craved the filial devotion. The more lonely he was, the more he depended on it . . . Yet at times Lyova's absolute devotion disturbed him: he wanted greater independence in his son and almost wished for some sign of dissent. But dissent, when there was a hint of it, upset him and made him fear estrangement.' In January 1931, they decided to separate for a while, and Lyova went to Berlin. He was now living with Jeanne Martin, the wife of Raymond Molinier, who had left her husband for Lyova: Molinier was a frequent visitor to Prinkipo, and some embarrassment may have been avoided by the departure of Lyova and Jeanne.

Lyova's place at Prinkipo was taken by Zina – who was unable to fill it. Of all Trotsky's children, it was she who resembled him most in appearance and temperament. Zina's husband, Platon Volkov, had been deported to Siberia in 1928, at the same time as Man Nevelson, the husband of her sister Nina. Both young women were ill with consumption – from which Nina died, at the early age of twenty-six. Zina, who had nursed her, survived – but the strain of this harrowing experience upset her mental balance, tinging her lively intelligence with a morbid neurosis. When she was allowed to leave Russia at the beginning of 1931, she came accompanied by Seva, her five-year-old son; she had been forced to leave her daughter in Leningrad with Alexandra, who was also taking care of Nina's two children. At Prinkipo, Zina could not conceal her resentment of Natalya, although the latter treated her with tact and affection. Trotsky, the supreme exponent of reason, was at a loss when confronted with irrational behaviour. He persuaded Zina, against her will, to go to Berlin for psychiatric treatment, leaving her child behind in Turkey. When they parted, Trotsky told her: 'You are an astonishing person. I have never met anyone like you.'

At Berlin Zina rejected the friendship of Lyova, whom she jealously considered her father's favourite. When Stalin deprived Trotsky of Soviet nationality in February 1932, all his family automatically became stateless political émigrés. Zina now felt more alone than ever, and sent for Seva; but he was stateless too, and could not travel. Later in the year, she wrote to her father: 'You act too impatiently and therefore sometimes impetuously. Do you know the meaning of something as complex and yet as elementary as instinct? . . . Who says that instinct is blind? . . . Instinct has terribly keen eyes which see in the dark . . . The doctors have only confused me . . . Do you know what sustained me? *Faith in you . . .* and is this not instinct?' Seva was finally allowed to join her in January 1933: she killed herself a week after his arrival. Shortly before, she had written to her mother: 'It is sad that I can no longer return to Papa. You know how I have adored and worshipped him from my earliest days. And now we are in utter discord. This has been at the bottom of my illness.' Grief-stricken, Alexandra told Trotsky in a letter: 'I explained to her that all this comes from your character, from the fact that you find it so difficult to show your feelings even when you would like to show them.' Alexandra reproached Trotsky for forcing psychiatric treatment on Zina when 'she was so closed in herself – as we both are – and one should not have pressed her to talk about things she did not want to talk about.' But she softened the blame in a tragic phrase: 'Our children were doomed.'

Lyova and Jeanne assumed responsibility for Seva, taking him with them to Paris when they had to escape from the Nazis in March 1933. Before leaving Berlin, Lyova had managed to get a telephone call through to Moscow in order to break the news of Zina's suicide to Sergei: this was the last time that the brothers were able to communicate. In April 1935, Trotsky wrote in his diary: 'Alexandra Lvovna Sokolovskaya, my first wife, who was living in Leningrad with my grandchildren, has been deported to Siberia . . . The letters from our younger son, Seryozha, professor in the Institute of Technology, have stopped. In the last one he wrote that certain dis-

Sergei Sedov (Seryozha) with Lyova's son in Moscow, 1934

turbing rumours were gathering around him... Seryozha, in contrast to . . . [Lyova] . . . and partly out of direct opposition to him, from the age of twelve or so turned his back on politics; he practised gymnastics, loved the circus, and even wanted to become a circus performer; later he took up technical subjects, worked hard, and became a professor; recently, in collaboration with two other engineers, he published a book on motors. If he has really been banished, there could be no political basis for it . . . Seryozha married early: he and his wife lived for several years in one room which was left to them in the last apartment we occupied after leaving the Kremlin. About a year and a half ago Seryozha and his wife were separated, but for lack of another room they continued to live there together . . . Perhaps Lelia has been deported too?' Natalya suffered agonies of anxiety about her younger son, but Trotsky noted that she was at first more troubled by the fate of Alexandra, who was now over sixty. Then, on 1 June, he wrote: 'Seryozha has been arrested; he is in prison; now it is no longer guesswork, something almost certain but not quite . . . He was arrested, evidently, about the time our correspondence stopped . . . Almost half a year has elapsed since that time . . . Poor boy . . . And my poor, poor Natasha . . .'

In the spring of 1935, uneasily aware that the French government might at any moment submit to pressure and enforce the existing expulsion order, Trotsky asked for asylum in Norway, where a Labour Party had recently come to power. This was granted, on condition that he refrain from political activity – a condition understood by Trotsky to apply only to Norwegian politics. He therefore left France for ever, arriving with Natalya at Oslo on 18 June, where a socialist editor called Konrad

Trotsky with Lyova at Barbizon in November 1933
Top: Leon Sedov (Lyova)

Knudsen invited him to live at his house in Vexhall, a village near Honnefoss, about thirty miles from the capital. Trotsky was run down in health, subject to persistent fevers, and in September he went into hospital at Oslo: the bills were high, and he could ill afford to pay them. But he had recovered by the end of the year, and was able to resume work on *The Revolution Betrayed*, which occupied him until the following August. This complex, difficult and important work contains his final analysis of the development of Soviet society, a diagnosis of its ills and a vision of its possible future. 'Bureaucratic autocracy must give place to Soviet democracy. A restoration of the right of criticism and genuine freedom of elections is the necessary condition for the further development of the country. This assumes a revival of freedom of Soviet parties, beginning with the party of the Bolsheviks, and a renascence of the trade unions . . . Free discussion of economic problems will decrease the overhead expense of bureaucratic mistakes . . . Expensive playthings – Palaces of the Soviets, new theatres, showy Metro subways – will be abandoned in favour of workers' dwellings . . . Ranks will be immediately abolished . . . Youth will receive the opportunity to breathe freely, criticize, make mistakes, and grow up. Science and art will be freed of their chains. And, finally, foreign policy will return to the traditions of revolutionary internationalism.'

Among the many subjects discussed in *The Revolution Betrayed* is that of the emancipation of women. 'How man enslaved woman, how the exploiter subjected them both, how the toilers have attempted at the price of blood to free themselves from slavery and have only exchanged one

Natalya, Trotsky and Jean van Heijenoort arriving at Oslo
Top: Trotsky on the boat from France to Norway
Right: Konrad Knudsen's house at Vexhall
Far right: the Soviet paper *Krokodil* accuses Trotsky of conspiring with the Nazis to overthrow the U.S.S.R.

chain for another – history tells us much about all this. In essence, it tells us little else.' He claims that the October Revolution honestly fulfilled its obligations to woman. 'The young government not only gave her all political and legal rights in equality with man, but, what is more important, did all that it could . . . actually to secure her access to all forms of economic and cultural work . . . The revolution made a heroic effort to destroy the so-called "family hearth" – that archaic, stuffy and stagnant institution in which the woman of the toiling classes performs galley labour from childhood to death.' But in this as in other ways, the revolution had been betrayed. 'The forty million Soviet families remain in their overwhelming majority nests of medievalism, female slavery and hysteria . . . feminine and childish superstition.'

№ 24 АВГУСТ   ИЗДАНИЕ ГАЗЕТЫ „ПРАВДА"   МОСКВА 1936

КРОКОДИЛ

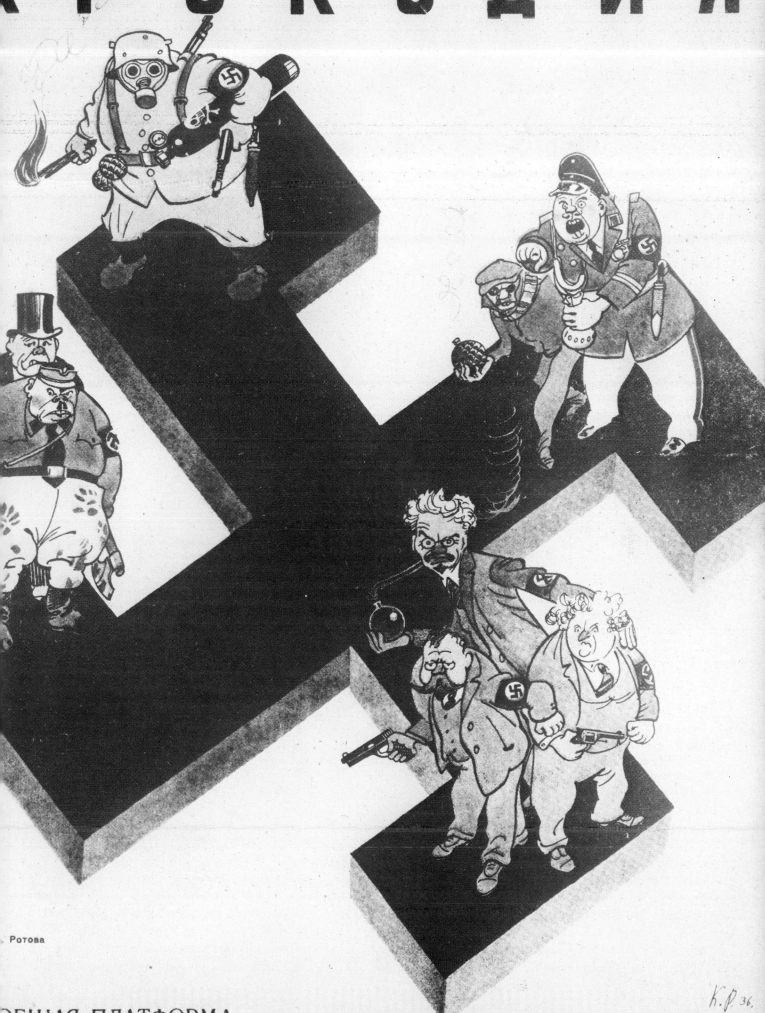

Ротова

ОБЩАЯ ПЛАТФОРМА

At first, police surveillance in Norway was comparatively unobtrusive. To appease some critics, the Minister of Justice, Trygve Lie, ordered the deportation of one of Trotsky's secretaries, Jan Fraenkel; he was soon replaced by Erwin Wolf, who married Knudsen's daughter. Events did not take a really sinister turn until August 1936. While Trotsky and Knudsen were away on a short holiday, members of Major Quisling's pro-Nazi party, the National Sammling, broke into the house at Vexhall and stole some of Trotsky's papers. A week later, it was announced over the radio that Zinoviev, Kamenev and fourteen other defendants were to stand trial in Moscow, accused of treason, conspiracy and attempts to assassinate Stalin. Trotsky was indicted as their chief associate, and Lyova named as his main assistant; it was also claimed that Trotsky, in collusion with the Gestapo, had been dispatching terrorists from Norway to the Soviet Union. This nightmare was even worse than any Trotsky had predicted. 'Terrorism? Terrorism?' he kept on repeating. 'Well, I can still understand this charge. But Gestapo?

Did they say Gestapo?' To quote Isaac Deutscher: 'His ears once more glued to the wireless set, he listened, from 19 to 24 August, to the accounts of the trial. Hour by hour he absorbed its horror, as prosecutor, judges and defendants acted out a spectacle so hallucinatory in its masochism and sadism that it seemed to surpass human imagination.'

Trotsky's frenzied attempts to rebut these fantastic accusations were frustrated on the first day after the trial, when he was asked to sign a document promising to abstain from even indirect interference in the politics of any other country. He indignantly refused, and was placed under house arrest. On 28 August, under heavy police escort, he appeared at the Oslo Court to give evidence in the case against Quisling's raiders. He was treated more as a defendant than a witness, and once more Trygve Lie commanded him to take what amounted to a vow of silence. When Trotsky again refused, Lie deported his secretaries and placed guards inside Knudsen's house, so that Trotsky could not communicate with its other inhabitants. On 2 September, he and Natalya were interned in a

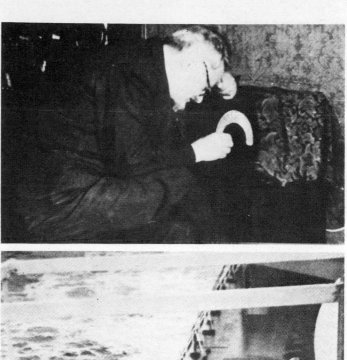

Bound for Mexico, Trotsky has his hair cut on the Norwegian tanker *Ruth* in December 1936
Top: Trotsky – 'ears glued to the wireless set'
Left: Trotsky with Erwin Wolf at the Oslo Court on 28 August 1936
Above left: Trotsky and Natalya with Norwegian comrades on a picnic in 1936

small house south of Oslo, by a remote fjord: they were now effectively cut off from the rest of the world. He was recalled as a witness in the Quisling trial on 11 December, and hoped for a chance to defend himself at last; but the court was emptied of press and public as soon as he took the stand. When Trygve Lie threatened to move his place of internment to an even more inaccessible spot in the far north, Trotsky remembered his friend Diego Rivera, the famous Mexican painter. Rivera easily persuaded the Mexican President, Lazaro Cardenas, to grant Trotsky asylum; Lie was only too pleased to be rid of him; and on 19 December Trotsky and Natalya set sail, alone but for their police escort, on the Norwegian tanker *Ruth*, bound for Tampico. He had left Europe for the last time.

The *Ruth* docked on 9 January, 1937. Max Shachtman and Diego Rivera's wife, Frida Kahlo, were waiting at the harbour to greet them. President Cardenas had sent a special train to take the new arrivals to a station near the capital, where they were warmly welcomed by Rivera who took them to his attractive home, the Blue House, in a suburb of Mexico City called Coyoacan. Rivera's ebullient and enthusiastic personality, and the atmosphere surrounding him of enlightened aesthetic appreciation, provided a pleasant contrast to the austerity of Trotsky's final months in Norway. A week later, he said in an interview: 'My next and most important task is the completion of my book about Lenin. I have already devoted two years to this work and I require another year or more in which to finish it. Lenin is now the most distorted, falsified and calumniated theoretician and revolutionary leader of our time. The machine of distortion and calumny is called the Comintern . . . In his book, *The State and Revolution*, and in other volumes, Lenin purged from the genuine teaching of Marx all the spurious ingredients introduced by the social democracy. I will try now in my book to purge the teachings of Lenin of the poisonous distortions and falsifications of the Soviet bureaucracy.' But his book on Lenin was never finished; more immediate falsifications by the bureaucracy distracted his attention and occupied his time.

The second Moscow trial opened a fortnight after Trotsky's arrival in Mexico. There were seventeen defendants, including Radek, Pyatakov and Nikolai Muralov. The charges were more outrageous than ever – Trotsky and Lyova were accused of having formed an alliance with Hitler and the Emperor of Japan to bring about the defeat of the Soviet Union – and the 'evidence' offered was so far-fetched that, given the time and the opportunity, much of it was easy to disprove. For instance, Pyatakov said that he had flown from Berlin to Oslo in December 1935 to receive instructions from Trotsky on methods of sabotage and revolt: but Trotsky had no difficulty in establishing irrefutable alibis for the whole of this period, and the Oslo Airport Authority issued a statement that no plane from Berlin had landed there throughout the relevant month. During the trial, Sergei Sedov was rearrested in Siberia and accused of attempting the mass poisoning of factory workers under orders from his father. Trotsky knew that Stalin would try to extract an incriminating confession from him: 'The GPU will not hesitate to drive Sergei to insanity and then they will shoot him.' Already, after his first arrest, the GPU had pressed Sergei to betray Trotsky; when he refused he was sentenced to five years in a labour camp. Here he met a number of Trotskyists, and after the first Moscow trial had joined them in a widespread hunger-strike which lasted for 132 days. Physically enfeebled by his fast, he was brought back to Moscow early in 1937 on the trumped-up 'poisoning' charge and submitted to even more rigorous 'interrogation'. But his grim experiences in Siberia had given the formerly unpolitical Sergei a new moral strength, and he withstood the ordeal. The details of his ultimate fate are unknown: it merged with that of

the anonymous millions who died, either by execution or through bodily exhaustion, in Stalin's concentration camps.

Trotsky undertook to establish a full alibi for the 'crimes' of which he and Lyova had been accused, and to answer in detail every single one of the charges. This seemed an impossible task: in some cases the very wildness of the lies made them difficult to refute, and a vast amount of research was necessary as evidence had to be gathered from innumerable sources in different and distant places. But Trotsky was determined to fight back: with few resources, either of money or manpower, at his disposal, and hampered by the comparative isolation of his situation in Mexico, he set about the supervision and organization of this daunting work with even more than his usual energy, aided by his phenomenal powers of memory and concentration. Committees In Defence Of Trotsky were formed in various countries; and in March 1937, those from the U.S.A., Great Britain, France and Czechoslovakia combined to form a Joint Commission of Inquiry. The idea was to conduct a counter-trial of Trotsky, in which he would be given the right to defend himself.

The Commission consisted of the following members: John Dewey, the distinguished American liberal philosopher; Otto Ruehle, the biographer of Karl Marx and former member of the Reichstag who, alone with Liebknecht, had voted against the First World War; two American journalists, Suzanne la Follette and Benjamin Stolberg; Carleton Beals, an authority on Latin-American affairs; Alfred Rosmer, who was the only member of the Commission to have been an associate of Trotsky's; Wendelin Thomas, a Communist member of

Natalya, Trotsky and Max Shachtman (in white hat) at Tampico on 9 January 1937
Left: Trotsky and Natalya (followed by Frida Kahlo Rivera) disembarking at Tampico
Top left: Natalya and Trotsky on arrival at Mexico

2c

TRU

ABOUT THE M

No. 1   NEW

TROTSKY
MOSCO

John Dewey Hea

Noted Publicists Hear Trotsky;
Stalinists Fear To Face Issue

A preliminary Commission of Inquiry headed by Dr. John Dewey, America's foremost liberal educator and philosopher, began this week in Mexico to take the testimony of Leon Trotsky as the first phase of the work of an international commission of inquiry into the Moscow trials.

The demand for an impartial commission of inquiry support

Published by
PIONEER PUBLISHERS
100 Fifth Ave., New York
Bundle orders $1 per 100.
Send checks or money
order with orders.

Editor: MAX SHACHTMAN

N. Y.   401   APRIL, 1937

BARES
W FRAUD

s *Mexico Inquiry*

DES NOT CONFESS!

ONLY TRUTH CAN UNMASK FRAME-UP

These pages seek to tell the
truth about the Moscow trials,
the most infamous frame-ups in

the Reichstag; Edward A. Ross, an American sociologist; John Chamberlain, an American literary critic; Carlo Tresca, an Italian anarchist; and a Mexican journalist, Francisco Zamora. A sub-committee, made up of Dewey, Beals, Ruehle, Stolberg and Miss La Follette, was sent to Coyoacan to hold a Preliminary Commission of Inquiry into the Charges Made Against Leon Trotsky In The Moscow Trials. Dewey was the Commission's Chairman, and Miss La Follette was its Secretary; John F. Finerty, who had defended Sacco and Vanzetti, acted as counsel for the Commission – in other words, as prosecuting attorney; and Trotsky's lawyer Albert Goldman was the counsel for his defence. Thirteen hearings were held in Trotsky's study at the Blue House between 10 April and 17 April. About fifty people were present in all, including the press and a few interested spectators. Two witnesses were called: Jan Fraenkel, the Czech who had been Trotsky's secretary in Turkey and Norway, and Leon Trotsky himself.

The hearings were conducted in English, putting Trotsky at a disadvantage which he triumphantly overcame; precision was all-important, and he attained it even through the barrier of a language in which he was not entirely at home. Thirty-four exhibits were put before the Commission to document the case. As the complicated proceedings wore on, with cross-examination following direct examination and tiny details of place and time acquiring a momentous significance, Trotsky grew increasingly tired but he never became confused. The transcript, published in book form as *The Case of Leon Trotsky*, gives a remarkably clear and full account of his political career and his personal life, as well as the ideas and beliefs which had governed both. Gradually, all of Stalin's accusations were proved to be factually untrue, and the motives behind them (which had bewildered so many of Trotsky's potential sympathizers) were carefully exposed.

'The formulas of Marxism, expressing the interests

**Left to right, Jean van Heijenoort, Albert Goldman, Trotsky, Natalya and Jan Fraenkel during the hearings of the Commission
Opposite page: nine of the defendants in the three Moscow trials**

A. Rykov

G. Zinoviev

L. Kamenov

K. Radek

N. Bukharin

H. Yagoda

N. Muralov

C. Rakovsky

N. Krestinsky

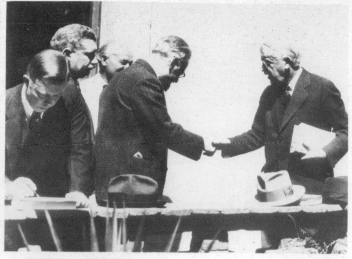

Trotsky with John F. Finerty, the 'prosecuting attorney'
Above: Trotsky (left) testifying to the Preliminary Commission.
John Dewey in the centre, with Suzanne La Follette on his left
Top: Trotsky shaking hands with Dr John Dewey
Right: during the hearings – left to right, John McDonald,
Albert Goldman, Jan Fraenkel, Jean van Heijenoort,
Riba Hansen and Ruth Agelof. McDonald was a visitor from
New York; Riba Hansen's husband Joseph was one of
Trotsky's secretaries in Mexico; Ruth Agelof was a temporary
secretary for the Dewey Commission

of the masses, more and more inconvenienced the bureaucracy, in so far as they were inevitably directed against its interests. From the time that I entered into opposition to the bureaucracy, its courtier-theoreticians began to call the revolutionary essence of Marxism – "*Trotskyism*". At the same time, the official conception of *Leninism* changed from year to year, becoming more and more adapted to the needs of the ruling caste. Books devoted to Party history, to the October Revolution, or the theory of Leninism, were revised annually. I have adduced an example from the literary activity of Stalin himself. In 1918 he wrote that the October insurrection was "principally and above all" assured by Trotsky's leadership. In 1924 Stalin wrote that Trotsky could not have played any special role in the October Revolution. To this tune the whole historiography was adjusted. This signifies in practice that hundreds of young scholars and thousands of journalists were systematically trained in the spirit of falsification. Whoever resisted was stifled. This applies in a still greater measure to the propagandists, functionaries, judges, not to speak of the examining magistrates of the GPU. The incessant Party purges were directed above all toward the uprooting of "Trotskyism", and during these purges not only discontented workers were called "Trotskyites", but also all writers who honestly presented historical facts or citations which contradicted the latest official standardization. Novelists and artists were subject to the same regime. The spiritual atmosphere of the country became completely impregnated with the poison of conventionalities, lies and direct frame-ups.

'All the possibilities along this road were soon exhausted. The theoretical and historical falsifications no longer attained their aims – people grew too accustomed to them. It was necessary to give to bureaucratic repression a more massive foundation. To bolster up the literary falsifications, accusations of a criminal character were brought in.

'My exile from the U.S.S.R. was officially motivated by the allegation that I had prepared an "armed insurrection". However, the accusation launched against me was not even published in the press. Today it may seem incredible, but already in 1929 we were confronted with accusations against the Trotskyites of "sabotage", "espionage", "preparation of railroad wrecks", etc, in the Soviet press. However, there was not a single trial

'Esteemed Commissioners! The experience of my life, in which there has been no lack either of successes or of failures, has not only not destroyed my faith in the clear, bright future of mankind, but, on the contrary, has given it an indestructible temper. This faith in reason, in truth, in human solidarity, which at the age of eighteen I took with me into the workers' quarters of the provincial Russian town of Nikolayev – this faith I have preserved fully and completely. It has become more mature, but not less ardent. In the very fact of your Commission's formation . . . I see a new and truly magnificent reinforcement of the revolutionary optimism which constitutes the fundamental element of my life.'

When he had finished, there was a silence, and then applause. John Dewey rose to speak: 'Anything I can say will be an anti-climax.' He adjourned the sessions of the Preliminary Commission, which, he pointed out, might be regarded 'as opening the investigation of the larger and complete Commission.' It was not until December 1937 that the International Commission reached its final conclusions and published its report. The verdict was contained in the last two sentences: 'We therefore find the Moscow Trials to be a frame-up. We therefore find Trotsky and Sedov not guilty.'

The French surrealist André Breton had long been one of Trotsky's most ardent admirers; he came to stay at the Blue House in February 1938. Long discussions between Breton, Rivera and Trotsky resulted in the *Manifesto: Towards A Free Revolutionary Art*, which was published later in the year over the signatures of Breton

A grim gallery compiled by Trotsky's followers in New York in March 1938
Above left: Trotsky is expunged from Soviet history.
In one of these photographs of Lenin speaking, Trotsky is shown standing at the foot of the steps. In the other, official version, taken within seconds, he is no longer there

involving these accusations. The matter was limited to a literary calumny which represented, nevertheless, the first link in the preparation of the future judicial frame-ups. To justify the repressions, it was necessary to have framed accusations. To give weight to the false accusations, it was necessary to reinforce them with more brutal repressions. Thus the logic of the struggle drove Stalin along the road of gigantic judicial amalgams.

'They also became necessary to him for international reasons. If the Soviet bureaucracy does not want revolutions and fears them, it cannot, at the same time, openly renounce the revolutionary traditions without definitely undermining its prestige within the U.S.S.R. However, the obvious bankruptcy of the Comintern opens the way for a new International. Since 1933, the idea of new revolutionary parties under the banner of the Fourth International has met with great success in the Old and New Worlds. Only with difficulty can an outside observer appreciate the real dimensions of this success. It cannot be measured by membership statistics alone. The general tendency of the development is of much greater importance . . . If Stalin fears the little *Bulletin of the Opposition* and punishes its introduction into the U.S.S.R. with death, it is not difficult to understand what fright seizes the bureaucracy at the possibility that news of the self-sacrificing work of the Fourth International in the service of the working class may penetrate into the U.S.S.R.'

Trotsky ended his final plea on a personal note:

and Rivera but which was almost entirely written by Trotsky. 'It is our deliberate will to keep to the formula: *any licence in art* . . . [But] in defending freedom of creation, we intend in no way to justify political indifference.' The *Manifesto*, which re-echoed ideas expressed in *Literature and Revolution* and other writings by Trotsky on the relationship between politics and art, urged the formation of an 'International Federation of Independent Revolutionary Art', and summarized its aims as: 'The independence of art – for the revolution. The revolution – for the complete liberation of art!' But the civilized pleasure taken by Trotsky in Breton's society was brutally shattered by news from Paris that overwhelmed both Natalya and himself in a greater grief than any they had so far had to bear.

Lyova had been living in a nightmare since the first Moscow trial had revealed that he was the GPU's main target after Trotsky. He had been warned by Ignaz Reiss, an important member of the Soviet secret service who had resigned his post and announced his adherence to the Fourth International, that Stalin was determined to liquidate Trotskyism by any means both inside and outside Russia. The warning was confirmed all too soon when Reiss's body, shot full of bullet-holes, was discovered lying on a roadside near Lausanne. Vulnerable, spied upon and lonely, Lyova had come to rely more and more on the friendship of a young man called Mark Zborowski, known in the Trotskyist movement as 'Etienne', who worked with him on the *Bulletin* in Paris. Gradually Lyova confided all his secrets to Etienne; his

Mexico, 1938: left to right, Diego Rivera, Frida Rivera, Natalya, Riba Hansen, André Breton, Trotsky, a Mexican comrade, a Mexican policeman, a Mexican driver and Jean van Heijenoort on an outing
Left: André Breton, Diego Rivera and Trotsky

trust and affection were to have fatal results. When part of Trotsky's archives, in Lyova's care, vanished after a mysterious burglary, he insisted that of all his associates Etienne at least was above suspicion. Debilitated in health, demoralized by worry and overwork, Lyova was finally persuaded by Etienne to enter a private clinic run by Russian émigrés and undergo a delayed operation for appendicitis. He made a quick recovery, and the only visitors to the clinic during his convalescence were Etienne and Jeanne. Then he suddenly suffered an

Trotsky and Natalya with two American visitors to Mexico
Above: table decoration designed by Diego Rivera to celebrate
Trotsky's fifty-eighth birthday – which was also the
anniversary of the October revolution – on 26 October 1937,
at the Blue House, Coyoacan

Trotsky in Mexico, at the Citadel, Teotihuacán
Top: Trotsky and Natalya on a visit to a Mexican farm
Right: Mexico, 1938 – left to right, Diego Rivera, Natalya,
Riba Hansen, André Breton, Frida Rivera, Jean van
Heijenoort; Trotsky in front

unexplained relapse, exhibiting all the symptoms of having been poisoned. He died, delirious and in agony, on 16 February 1938. His highly responsible position in the Trotskyist organization was then filled by Etienne. Twenty years later, Etienne confessed that he had been an agent for Stalin; he had replaced Sobolevicius when the latter began to arouse suspicion, and had succeeded in penetrating into the heart of the Trotskyist movement.

Trotsky composed a memorial to his son which is more moving than anything else he wrote. *Leon Sedov – Son, Friend, Fighter* recounts the facts of Lyova's brief life, suggests the reasons for his death, and pays tribute to his selfless dedication to revolutionary politics. Starting on a note of barely restrained emotion, it reaches an exalted climax: 'His mother – who was closer to him than any other person in the world – and I are living through these terrible hours recalling his image, feature by feature, unable to believe that he is no more and weeping because it is impossible not to believe. How can we accustom ourselves to the idea that upon this earth there no longer exists the warm, human entity bound to us by such indissoluble threads of common memories, mutual understanding and tender attachment? No one knew us and no one knows us, our strong and our weak sides, so well as he did. He was part of both of us, our young part. By hundreds of channels our thoughts and feelings daily reached out to him in Paris. Together with our boy has died everything that still remained young within us. Good-bye, Leon, good-bye dear and incomparable friend. Your mother and I never thought, never expected that destiny would impose on us this terrible task of writing your obituary. We lived in firm conviction that long after we were gone you would be the continuer of our common cause. But we were not able to protect you. Good-bye Leon! We bequeath your irreproachable memory to the younger generation of the workers of the world. You will rightly live in the hearts of all those who work, suffer and struggle for a better world. Revolutionary youth of all countries! Accept from us the memory of our Leon, adopt him as your son – he is worthy of it – and let him henceforth participate invisibly in your battles, since destiny has denied him the happiness of participating in your final victory.'

A month after Lyova's death, Stalin inaugurated the third and bloodiest of the Moscow trials. The twenty-one defendants included Bukharin, Rykov, Rakovsky, Nikolai Krestinsky and Henrikh Yagoda. Once more, Trotsky was denounced as the arch-conspirator, this time with the Bukharinists, who had been among his greatest enemies. Once more, the lunatic accusations were succeeded by humiliating 'confessions'. And once more, Trotsky set about exposing 'the greatest frame-up in history', defiantly diagnosing the trials as merely a symptom, however murderous, of the death agony of the Soviet bureaucracy. 'The struggle between bureaucracy and society becomes more and more intense. In this struggle victory will inevitably go to the people . . .' Over the next few months, he worked on a pamphlet called *The Death Agony of Capitalism and the Tasks of the Fourth*

Trotsky (standing on the left) with friends in Mexico. Natalya is seated on the left, with Frida Rivera beside her and Ruth Agelof on the extreme right. Frida's face has been scratched out by Natalya – an indication of her feelings two years after the photograph was taken

International, which became known as *The Transitional Programme*. 'The Fourth International, already today, is deservedly hated by the Stalinists, Social Democrats, bourgeois liberals and fascists. There is not and there cannot be a place for it in any of the People's Fronts. It uncompromisingly gives battle to all political groupings tied to the apron-strings of the bourgeoisie. Its task – the abolition of capitalism's domination. Its aim – socialism. Its method – the proletarian revolution.' Trotsky's programme was formally adopted at the Foundation Congress of the Fourth International in September. He could not attend the meeting, which took place in France; and in his absence, the chief spokesman representing the Russian section was none other than Etienne.

Early in 1939, a quarrel broke out between the Trotskys and the Riveras: there were both political and personal reasons for this. Rivera's hatred of Stalinism had led him to come out in open support of a candidate for the extreme right wing in the Mexican Presidential elections,

Lyova, 1906–1938

and to accuse Lazaro Cardenas – who had behaved so hospitably to Trotsky – of being an accomplice of Stalin. Trotsky could not condone such an unbalanced excess of Stalinophobia, and felt that he should make a public break with Rivera. Meanwhile, relations between Natalya and Frida Rivera had become unpleasantly strained. For the first time since she had shared her life with Trotsky, Natalya found herself tormented by jealousy – possibly not altogether without reason, as Frida was an unusually beautiful woman. She was also a gifted artist, whose paintings reveal a morbid imagination and a destructive, even suicidal temperament. Natalya's uncontrollable dislike of her hostess was accompanied by remorse, which she tried to appease by embarrassingly demonstrative gestures of affection; these irritated Frida, whose cold reaction only increased Natalya's resentment. By the end of March, Trotsky and Natalya had moved into another house at Coyoacan, in the Avenida Viena, a convenient distance from the Rivera *ménage*. This became known as their 'little fortress': a watchtower was built over the entrance, the doors were heavily barred, a complicated alarm system was installed, five guards patrolled the exterior and double that number were always on duty inside.

In July, Alfred Rosmer and his wife Marguerite arrived at the Avenida Viena, where they stayed until the following May. Trotsky was happy to see these old friends, with whom he shared memories dating back to Paris in 1915, and even happier because they brought Seva with them. After Lyova's death, Trotsky had written to Jeanne Martin begging her to bring Seva over to Mexico. Jeanne, who had become passionately attached to the child, stubbornly refused either to accompany him there or to send him on his own. Lyova's life with Jeanne had not been happy. They had belonged to two different groups among the warring Trotskyist factions in Paris – he to the orthodox sect, and she to the splinter group that had formed round her ex-husband, Raymond Molinier, when he had quarrelled with Trotsky in 1935. In this atmosphere of suspicion and intrigue, Jeanne had become progressively hysterical. Trotsky – once again at sea in the face of unreason – embarked on a painfully squalid law-suit to regain possession of his grandson; but even when the courts had twice found in his favour, she still would not relinquish the boy.

Natalya, Trotsky and Seva, 1939
Top: Alfred and Marguerite Rosmer, 1939

The house in the Avenida Viena

Instead, she took him away with her to a secret destination. After a long search, Marguerite Rosmer discovered the hiding-place, and separated Seva from Jeanne; but a further attempt to abduct him was made by Jeanne's allies before the Rosmers were able to get him safely to his grandparents at Coyoacan.

At about four o'clock in the morning of 24 May 1940, Trotsky and Natalya were awakened by the sound of machine-gun fire just outside their bedroom. She helped him to the floor, pushing him into the space between the wall and the bed, and he dazedly whispered to her to lie down beside him. Some two hundred shots

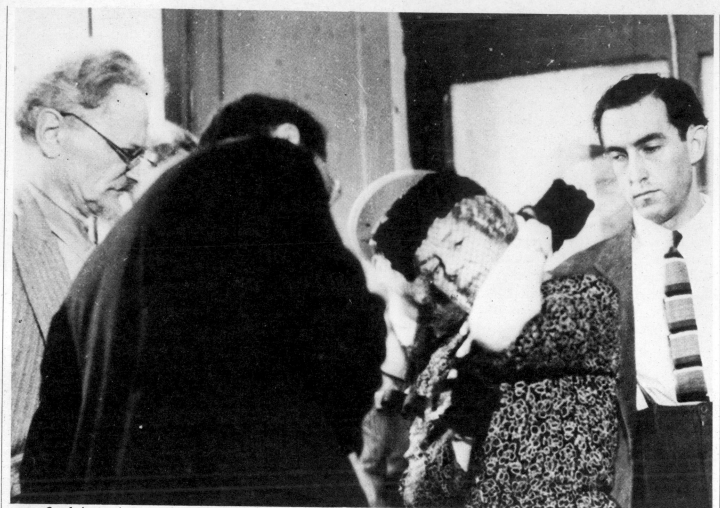

were fired into the room, half of which hit the area around their hiding-place: both were very slightly wounded. Then came silence, broken by the pathetic sound of Seva crying 'Grandpa!' from his room next door. The child's bedroom had been set on fire by an incendiary grenade, and by the light of the flames Natalya glimpsed the figure of a man on the threshold between the two rooms. He fired a last volley in the direction of their beds, and disappeared. While more shots could be heard further away, they ran into Seva's burning room: it was empty, and a trail of blood led out of it into the patio. The ominous silence was once more broken by Seva's voice from the patio, confidently calling to Alfred and Marguerite Rosmer; he had first hidden under his bed, and had been wounded in the toe. The guards inside the house now burst from their rooms and the whole household assembled excitedly in the courtyard. The Mexican police sentries had been disarmed and were found lying helplessly bound outside; the American guard on duty, Robert Sheldon Harte, had vanished. A clumsily made but potentially destructive bomb, which had not yet exploded, was discovered on the premises.

The raiding party had consisted of twenty-five men. Of the five police guards on duty, three had been asleep, and the officer in charge of them, J. Rodriguez Casas, claimed that he was at home in bed at the time of the attack. The raiders had apparently been admitted by Sheldon Harte, and when they had left (some of them stealing two of Trotsky's cars) they had taken him with them. Colonel Sanchez Salazar, Chief of the Mexican Secret Police, was called in; from the start he was puzzled by the whole affair. Both Trotsky and Natalya struck him as unnaturally calm after their ordeal – and Trotsky seemed almost triumphant. When Salazar asked him whom he suspected of having organized the attempt, he received the decisive answer: 'The author of the attack is Joseph Stalin, through the medium of the GPU.' Salazar then reached the conclusion that it had all been a put-up job, organized by Trotsky himself in order to discredit Stalin. He ignored Trotsky's suggestion that he might profitably interrogate some of the leading Mexican communists about the episode, and instead arrested three domestic servants and two of Trotsky's secretaries, Otto Schuessler and Charles Cornell.

Salazar's suspicions at first seemed to be partly confirmed by the equivocal behaviour of Harte, who had not only admitted the raiders but had also left in their company. It was not until 25 June that the young American's corpse was discovered buried in a lime pit near a farm outside the city; the farmhouse had been rented by two brothers, Luis and Leopoldo Arenal. Rumours that Harte may himself have been a GPU agent persisted, but Trotsky angrily rejected them. He pointed out that seven of his former secretaries had already been murdered by Stalin; that Harte had been a trusted friend, and that if he had really been an agent he could have easily stabbed Trotsky on the quiet without resorting to the complicated commotion of a mass attack. He erected a plaque in his garden commemorating 'Robert Sheldon Harte, 1915–1940, Murdered By Stalin'.

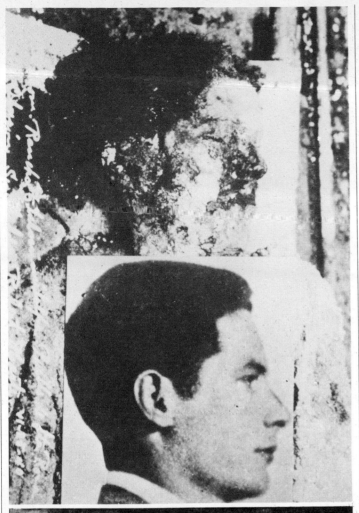

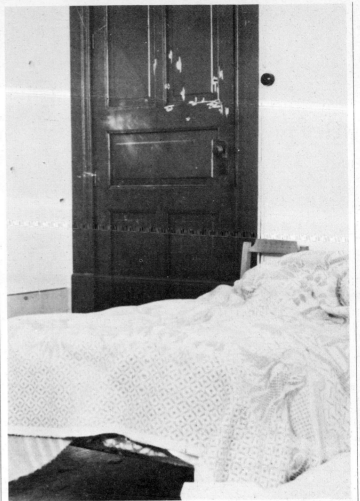

The memorial to Robert Sheldon Harte
Top: police identification photographs of Sheldon Harte before and after death
Top right: Trotsky's bedroom, riddled with bullet-holes after the Siqueiros raid
Top left: Trotsky watches as Natalya shows the police a wound she received in the raid

By this time, Salazar had succeeded in solving the case. The first clue emerged through a conversation he overheard while drinking in a bar. Apparently a Mexican magistrate had recently been drunkenly boasting that he had been asked to lend two policeman's uniforms to a man connected with the assault. Through the magistrate, Salazar traced this man, who in turn led him to the house of David Serrano. Serrano had already run away, but a search of the premises uncovered a document incriminating a certain Nestor Sanchez Hernandez. It was Hernandez who revealed the whole story to Salazar. Trotsky was proved triumphantly right; the raid had been the work of a vast network of Mexican Stalinists, many of them GPU agents, and some of them highly respected members of the community.

The leader of the raid was the celebrated Mexican painter, David Alfaro Siqueiros – a swashbuckling figure who had fought heroically in the Spanish Civil War and had been in the service of the GPU since 1928. On the night of the attack he had dressed up in the uniform of a major in the Mexican army, disguising himself under a false moustache and dark glasses: the whole enterprise had the faintly ludicrous aspect of an adventure story for boys. Behind Siqueiros there had been a shadowy presence, who kept himself in the background throughout, known variously to the other conspirators as 'Felipe' or 'the French Jew'. Siqueiros' wife, Angelica Arenal, had been deeply involved, as had her brothers Luis and Leopoldo. Another well-known painter, Antonio Pujol, had installed Serrano's wife, Julia Barrados, with a girl named Ana Lopez, in rooms near the Avenida Viena; it had been their assignment to seduce the police guards outside Trotsky's house and to report on any domestic details that they might learn. Ana Lopez's lover had provided the information which led the police to the discovery of Sheldon Harte's body. On 17 June, Salazar arrested twenty-seven people suspected of having been participants in the raid or involved in its planning: but Siqueiros, Pujol and the Arenals had escaped from

David Alfaro Siqueiros led the raid

Julia Barrados de Serrano seduced the guard

Angelica Arenal acted as an accomplice

Antonio Pujol helped to organize the raid

Nestor Sanchez Hernandez confessed to the police

Mexico, while no trace at all could be found of the mysterious 'Felipe'.

Siqueiros was not arrested until October. At the trial he admitted that he had taken part in the raid, but denied that the Communist Party had been involved or that he had intended to kill Trotsky. His aim, he said, had been merely to protest against Trotsky's presence in Mexico. The accused were acquitted of homicide, attempted homicide, use of firearms, criminal conspiracy and usurpation of official functions. Some relatively minor charges (house-breaking, unlawful use of police uniforms, robbery and damage to property) remained to be heard when Siqueiros, released on bail, disappeared from Mexico once more. He returned several years later and lives there still, where he continues to be regarded as one of the country's most distinguished citizens.

The disturbance of the raid, and his indignation at the reluctance of the authorities to recognize its origin and motive, did not prevent Trotsky from continuing to write. Apart from polemics inspired by the raid itself (*Stalin Seeks My Death*), he was at work on a full-scale book called *Stalin – An Appraisal Of The Man And His Influence*, and at the same time producing numerous articles on various aspects of the international situation. There was plenty to occupy his attention in this. With the signing of the Hitler-Stalin pact and the outbreak of the Second World War – events which Trotsky had been predicting throughout the 1930s – a conflict had arisen within the ranks of the Trotskyist group in New York. Two leading members of the Socialist Workers' Party, James Burnham and Max Shachtman, maintained that the Fourth International should cease to defend the Soviet Union against Imperialist countries; it was no longer possible to regard it as a workers' state, they considered, and concluded that it was essentially no different now from any other Imperialist power. Trotsky himself vehemently dismissed this reasoning as hysterical Stalinophobia, and insisted that his followers should continue to defend unconditionally the 'gains of October' against all foreign capitalist governments: the Soviet Union, in his opinion, was still a workers' state, in however degenerated a form. This subtle position was typical of Trotsky both in its stubborn moral integrity (given his loathing of both Stalinism and the Nazis) and in the vigour with which it was expressed. During the period between September 1939 and May 1940 the controversy became increasingly bitter, with a majority of American Trotskyists, led by James P. Cannon, accepting Trotsky's line, and a minority supporting the dissident Burnham and Shachtman. The split has never been resolved, and Trotskyist groups today are still divided between those who interpret the Soviet régime as a form of State Capitalism, and those who perpetuate Trotsky's own loyal definition of it as a degenerated workers' state.

Early one May morning, shortly after the Siqueiros raid, Trotsky was feeding his pet rabbits when a young man entered the courtyard from the street and shyly introduced himself as Frank Jacson. Trotsky had

Trotsky in his study at work on *Stalin*

Trotsky feeding his rabbits in the patio at Coyoacan

not met him before but recognized the name. Little was known about Jacson beyond the fact that he was the lover of a young American Trotskyist called Sylvia Agelof, and that through Sylvia he had become friendly with the Rosmers. He was vaguely assumed to be in Mexico City on business, and had called at the Avenida Viena several times over the past few weeks, sometimes bringing sweets for Natalya or a toy for Seva. He now explained that he had come to drive the departing Rosmers to Vera Cruz; Trotsky invited him to join them for breakfast. Jacson paid about ten more visits throughout the summer and became well known to the guards; but he only saw Trotsky two or three times. On one of these occasions he tactfully let it be known that he agreed with Trotsky on the question of the split in the Fourth International, although Sylvia had sided with Burnham and Shachtman; and in August he asked Trotsky to read an article he had written on the subject. They spent ten minutes together in the study, during which time Jacson sat behind Trotsky, wearing a hat and with an overcoat covering his arm which he kept pressed to his side. The article turned out to be confused, almost incoherent; Trotsky suddenly felt uneasy, and the following evening told Natalya that he did not want to see Jacson again.

At about half past five in the afternoon of the next day, 20 August 1940, Natalya stepped out on to the balcony and saw Trotsky again feeding his rabbits in the patio. Standing beside him was an unfamiliar figure. When the stranger approached her and took off his hat, she recognized him as Jacson: he had brought a corrected and typewritten copy of his article for Trotsky's approval. He asked her for a glass of water, as he was desperately thirsty; she offered him tea, but he said that he had lunched late and felt that the food was choking him. His face was grey and he seemed very nervous. When she asked why he had brought an overcoat on a fine day, he muttered something evasive about the possibility of rain. She then inquired after Sylvia, and he did not seem to understand her. As Natalya and Jacson joined Trotsky, the latter said to her in Russian: 'He is expecting Sylvia to call here. They are leaving tomorrow.' This was a suggestion that she should invite them to supper. Surprised, she explained that Jacson had refused tea and was feeling unwell. Trotsky looked at him carefully and said: 'Your health is poor, you look ill. That is not good . . .' There was a pause. Trotsky was visibly reluctant to leave the rabbits and in no mood for the article: however, he methodically closed the rabbit hutches, took off his working gloves, brushed off his blue blouse and slowly, silently, walked with Jacson into the house.

Assassination

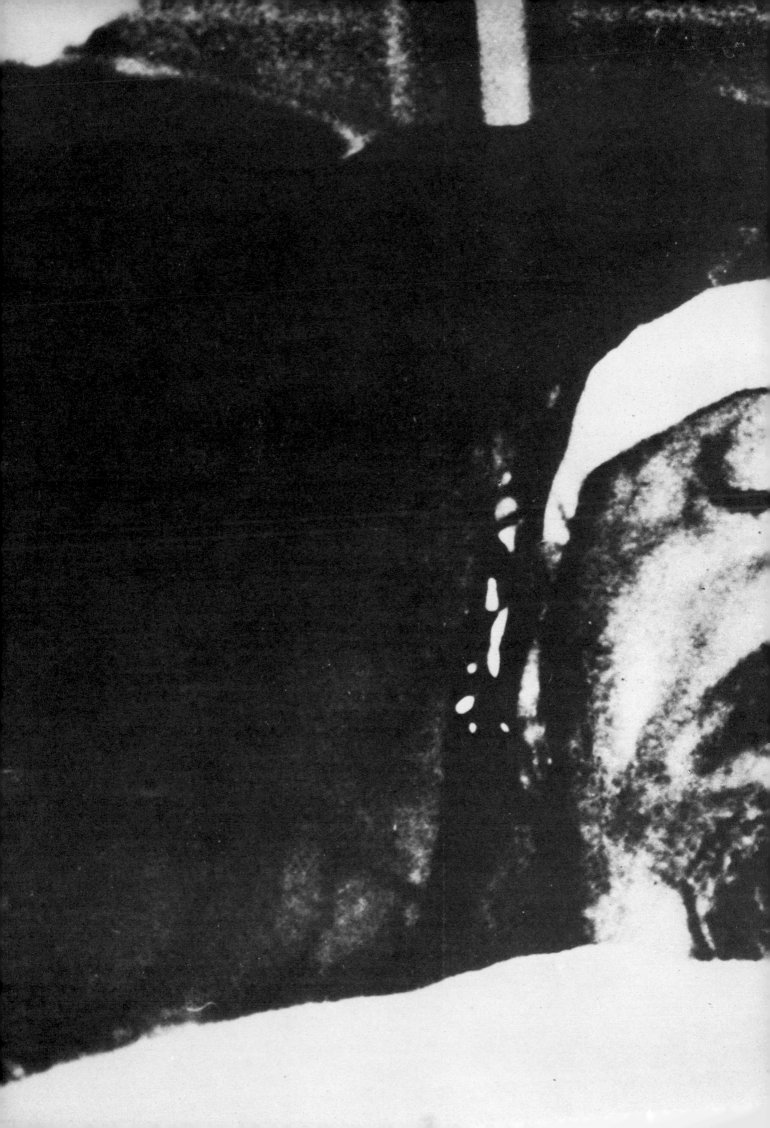

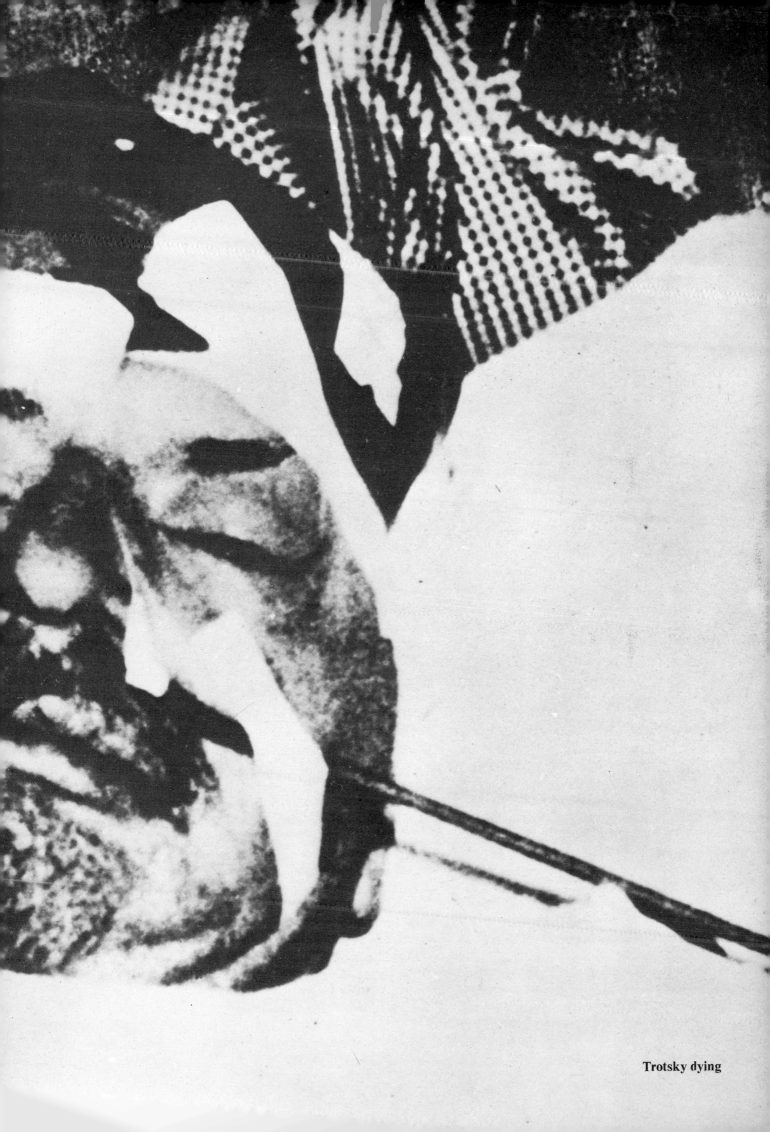

Trotsky dying

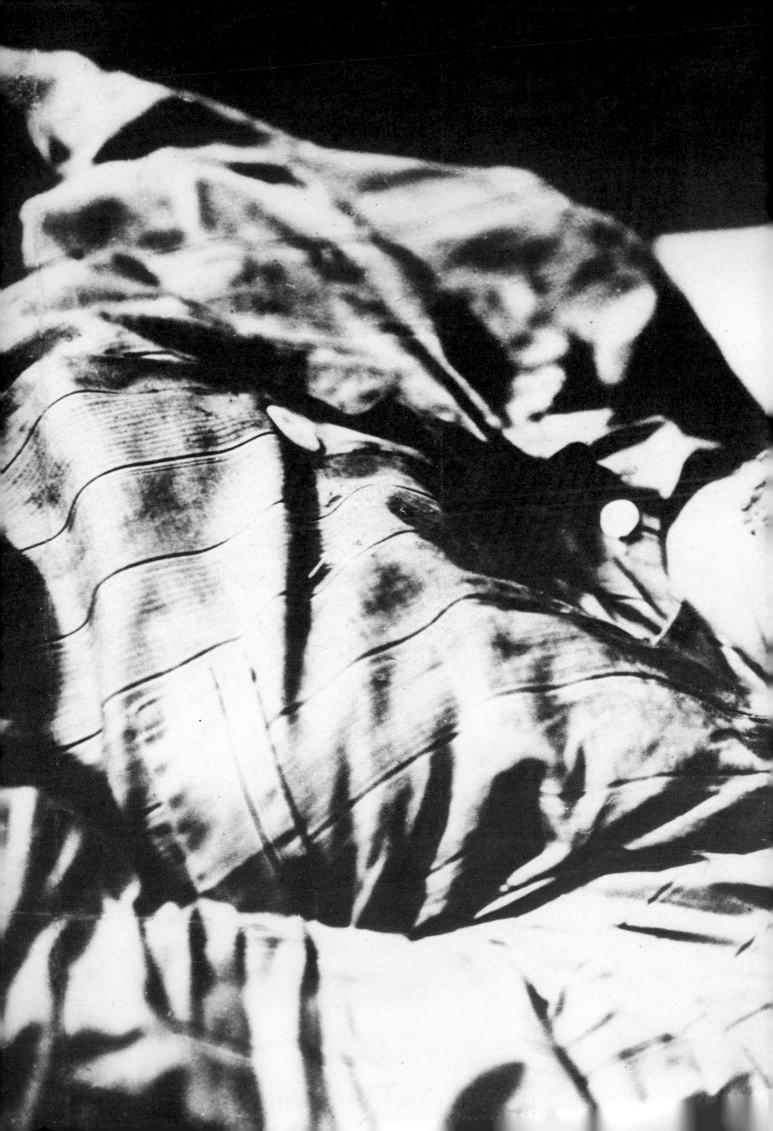

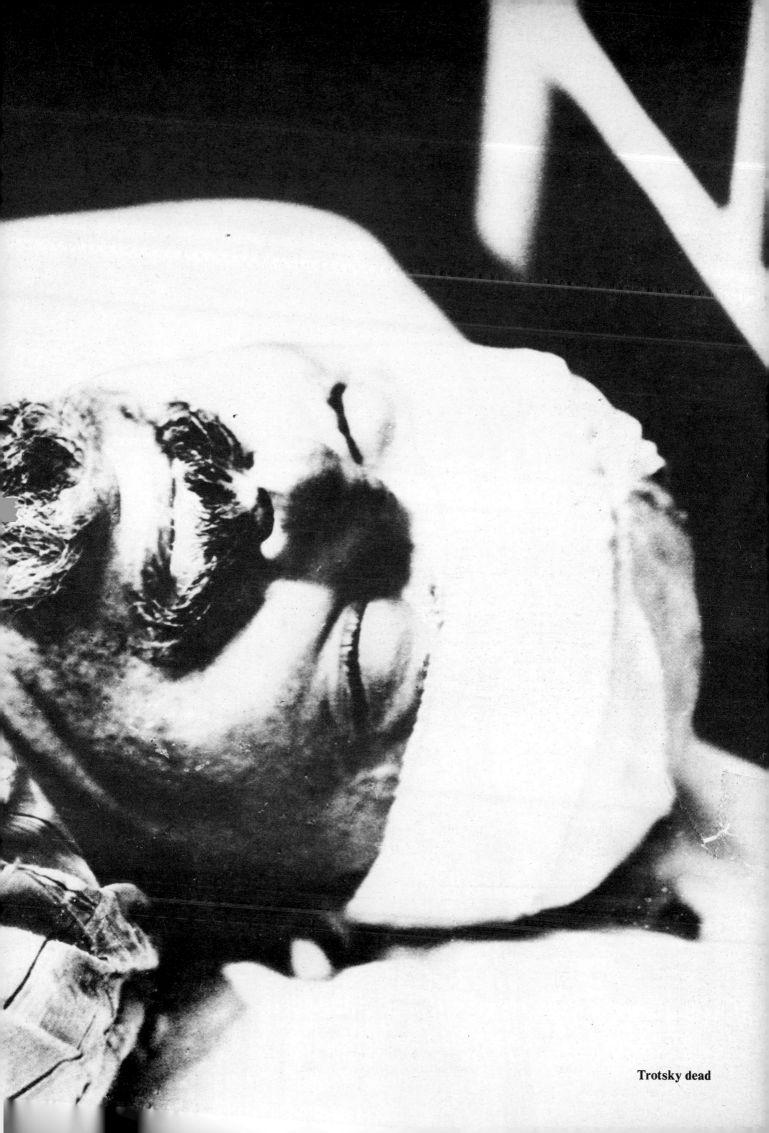

Trotsky dead

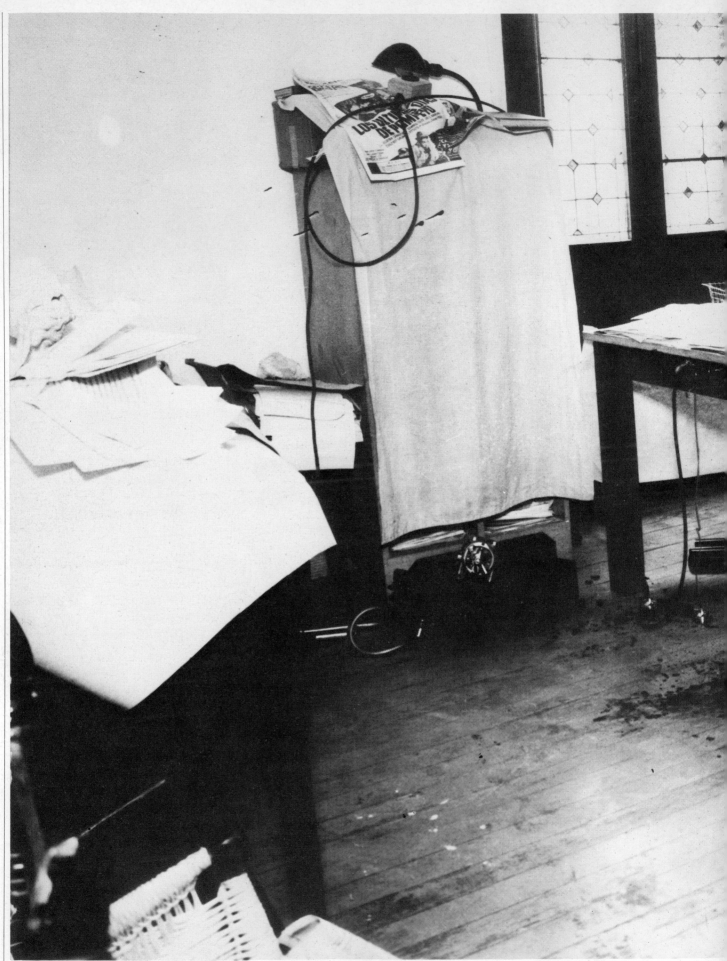

A few minutes after Trotsky had entered his study with Jacson, the room was covered in their blood: the assassin's ̶
spattered all over the floor, while the victim's had fallen on the desk where it stained the pages of his unfinished biograp̶
of Stalin . . . At the critical moment three secretary-guards, Joseph Hansen, Charles Cornell and Melquiades Benitez, we̶
on the roof near the main guard tower, connecting a new siren with the alarm system in preparation for the GPU's ne̶

tack. They had seen Jacson arrive below in his car: he had waved to them and called out 'Is Sylvia here yet?' Cornell had ¬erated the electric controls on the double doors, and Harold Robins had admitted Jacson into the patio. Fifteen minutes ¬ssed before a terrible cry was heard – prolonged and agonized, half scream and half sob. Benitez aimed a rifle at the study ¬ndow, through which Trotsky could be glimpsed struggling with Jacson, but Hansen shouted 'Don't shoot! You might hit the Old Man!' Leaving Cornell and Benitez on the roof to cover the exits from the study, Hansen switched on the alarm and slid down the ladder to the library. As he ran into the dining-room, Trotsky stumbled out of the study a few feet away, blood streaming down his face. 'See what they have done to me!' he said. At the same moment, Robins rushed into the dining-room, followed by Natalya.

When Natalya heard the cry, she did not immediately realize who had uttered it, but hurried in the direction from which it had come. She saw Trotsky leaning against the doorpost between the dining-room and the balcony. His hands were hanging by his sides; his bright blue eyes were without their glasses; his face was covered in blood. Crying 'What happened? What happened?' she flung her arms around him; but he did not answer at once. For a moment she thought that he might have been accidentally injured by some repair work in the study. Then he said the one word 'Jacson' – but with no indignation in his voice, as if he meant to say 'It has happened at last.' He took a few steps and then collapsed on the floor. As she knelt beside him she heard him say 'Natasha, I love you.' He continued to speak with difficulty. 'Seva must be taken away from all this . . . You know, *in there*, I sensed . . . I

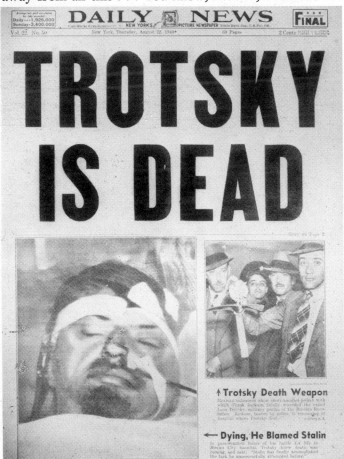

The assassination makes headline news
Right: detectives display the murder weapon

understood what he wanted to do . . . He wanted to strike me once more . . . but I didn't let him . . .'

Hansen and Robins had burst into the study, where they found Jacson with a revolver dangling limply from his hand. He was swaying, gasping, his face contorted. Robins sprang on him and brought him to the ground. Writhing beneath the attack, Jacson said 'They made me do it . . .' Hansen ran back to Trotsky and knelt beside him. Trotsky turned and spoke to him in English: 'We

talked about French statistics . . . Jacson shot me with a revolver. I am seriously wounded. I feel that this time it is the end.' When Hansen told him that he had not been shot, but struck with some instrument, he seemed unconvinced. A whimpering noise, and the sound of a renewed struggle, came from the study. 'Tell the boys not to kill him,' Trotsky whispered urgently. '*He must talk.*'

Cornell was sent to fetch a doctor who lived nearby. He intended to use Jacson's Buick but could not find the keys in it, so a frantic search was made for them in the assassin's clothes. As Jacson regained consciousness, he moaned: 'They have imprisoned my mother . . . Sylvia has nothing to do with this . . . No, it was not the GPU – I have nothing to do with the GPU . . .' The keys were not on him, and there was further delay while the garage doors were opened before Cornell left in another car. Meanwhile, Natalya had wiped the blood from Trotsky's face and put ice on his forehead; he continually touched her hand with

A grisly reconstruction of the crime by the Mexican police

his lips. 'Take care of Natalya,' he said to Hansen. 'She has been with me many, many years.' Hansen tried to reassure him that the wound was not serious. 'No,' he answered, and touched his heart: 'I feel *here* that this time they have succeeded.' When the doctor arrived, his left arm and leg were already paralysed. A few moments later, an ambulance came to take him to hospital and the police broke into the study to arrest the murderer.

In the ambulance, Trotsky made a tentative, restless movement with his right hand, as if searching for something; at last it came to rest in Natalya's. He whispered to her that he felt better. Then he gave Hansen instructions on how to conduct the investigation. He told him that Jacson was a political assassin, most likely an agent of the GPU but possibly a fascist aided by the Gestapo. A large crowd was waiting outside the hospital: Natalya was terrified that Trotsky, so vulnerable on his unattended stretcher, might be the victim of yet another assault. He was laid on a narrow bed and examined by more doctors. When a nurse cut his hair, he made a joking reference to the fact that he had intended to see the barber the day before. With an enormous effort, he dictated a message in broken English to Hansen: 'I am close to death from the blow of a political assassin . . . struck me down in my room. I struggled with him . . . we . . . entered . . . talk about French statistics . . . he struck me . . . Please say to our friends . . . I am sure . . . of the victory . . . of the Fourth International . . . Go forward . . .'

The wound was X-rayed and a decision was taken to operate. He insisted that Natalya, rather than a nurse, should undress him in preparation for this. She kissed his lips, and he returned the kiss. At about half past seven, he fell into a coma. Five surgeons operated on his skull; he bore the ordeal with extraordinary strength, but he never regained consciousness. He died at twenty-five minutes past seven in the evening of the following day.

The police had established that the murder weapon

was a mountaineer's ice-pick which Jacson had concealed in a pocket of his khaki raincoat, attached to it by a cord. The handle had been sawn off; the wooden stock was about a foot long and the steel head was about seven inches from tip to tip. One edge was sharp and the other was a fork-shaped hammer claw. Sewn into the lining of the coat they discovered an alternative weapon – a dagger measuring about fourteen inches, in a brown sheath embroidered with silver threads. He had also carried a ·45 calibre Star automatic pistol in the hip pocket of his trousers, with eight bullets in the magazine and one in the firing chamber.

Jacson's earlier visit to the study had been a 'dress-rehearsal' for the killing: he knew that Trotsky would sit at his desk to read the article, and on both occasions Jacson placed himself behind him, to the left, where he could prevent his victim from reaching the alarm switch. He may not have known that Trotsky had two guns of his own in the room, one only a few inches from his hand. Jacson gave the police a detailed description of the final act: 'I put my raincoat on the table so that I could take the ice-pick out of the pocket. I decided to take advantage of

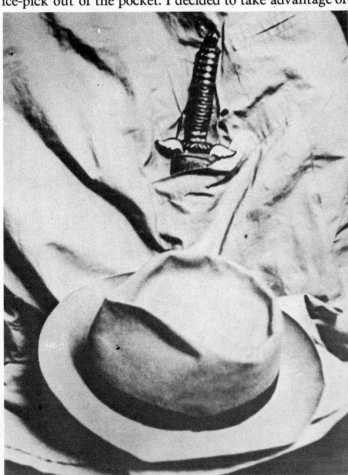

The assassin's hat, coat and dagger

the wonderful opportunity offered me and at the exact moment when Trotsky started to read my article I took the ice-pick out of the coat, took it in my fist and, closing my eyes, gave him a tremendous blow on the head . . . The man screamed in such a way that I will never forget it as long as I live. His scream was *Aaaa* . . . very long, infinitely long and it still seems to me as if that scream were piercing my brain. I saw Trotsky get up like a madman. He threw himself at me and bit my hand – look, you can still see the marks of his teeth . . . Then I pushed him, so that he fell to the floor. He lifted himself as best he could and then, running or stumbling, I don't know how, he got out of the room.'

After his arrest, an open letter of confession, written in French and covering three closely typed pages, was found on Jacson's person. In this unconvincing document he represented himself as belonging to an old Belgian family. In Paris – so the story went – he had become a fervent Trotskyist, and a member of the Fourth International had provided him with false papers and money in order to travel to Mexico and meet Trotsky face to face. The letter then described his gradual disillusionment in 'the Old Man'. Trotsky was once again falsely accused of all the familiar crimes: he had (so the letter maintained) asked Jacson to visit Russia in order to organize attacks on the lives of various people, including Stalin himself; he had accepted backing from the ultra-right-wing Dies Committee, which was conducting an anti-Communist witch-hunt in the U.S.A.; and he was plotting the murder of several leading Mexican politicians. To these routine libels, recognizably originating in the Kremlin, Jacson added another with a more personal touch: Trotsky, he claimed, had disgusted him by urging him to break with Sylvia – 'whom I love with all my soul' – because she had sympathized with the dissident group of Trotskyists led by Burnham and Shachtman.

Under police interrogation, Jacson filled in more details of his fictional biography. His real name, he said, was Jacques Mornard, and he had been born on 17 February, 1904, at Teheran, where his father was the Belgian ambassador. He had moved to Brussels at the age of two, and had spent the war years with his mother, Henriette Vandendreschd. After matriculating at a Jesuit college in Brussels, he spent two years at a military academy and then returned to Paris for further study. He later enrolled in a school of journalism, and had worked for the paper *Ce Soir* from 1930 to 1939. His father had died in 1926, and his mother supplied him with money; he had a brother called Robert who was in the Diplomatic Service. In 1934 he had married Henriette van Proudschdt in Brussels, but had left her after three months and divorced her in 1939.

All of this was categorically disproved when the real Jacques Mornard, who was indeed a Belgian journalist, cabled the Mexican authorities to establish his separate identity. But it was true enough that 'Jacson', under the name of Jacques Mornard, had met Sylvia Agelof in Paris during the summer of 1938, had become her lover and had promised to marry her 'at the right moment'. It was also

Harold Robins, captain of the guard at Avenida Viena

true that he had accompanied her to the Foundation Congress of the Fourth International, held at Alfred Rosmer's house near Paris on 3 September 1938: she had acted as an interpreter, and he had kept discreetly in the background. Sylvia had returned to New York in February 1939, and he had joined her there in September. He told her that he was the American correspondent for a Belgian newspaper, and explained that in order to avoid military service at home he was travelling with a false Canadian passport under the name of Frank Jacson. He seemed totally uninterested in the political activities which engrossed her. In October he announced that he was leaving for Mexico City as commission agent for an import-export firm. She followed him there in February,

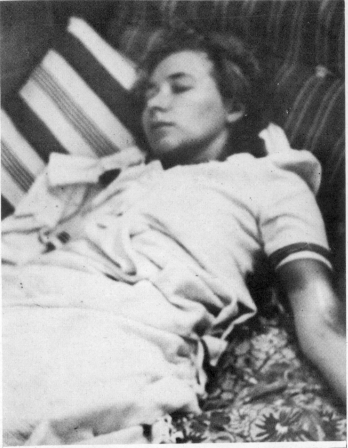

Outside the American Express in Paris, 1938: Sylvia Agelof (right) with Maria, the wife of Yvan Craipeau (centre)
Top and right: two pictures of Sylvia prostrate with grief after learning that her hero had been murdered by her lover

and although she tried to keep him away from Trotsky's household she could not avoid introducing him to her friends the Rosmers, to whom he went out of his way to be pleasant. Thus, by subtle and gradual stages, he had gained entry to the closely guarded Avenida Viena – unsuspected by everyone but Sylvia, who was disturbed by numerous inconsistencies in his behaviour and his history, but too much in love with him to probe deeper.

At the time of her first meeting with Jacson-Mornard, Sylvia Agelof was twenty-eight – a moderately good-looking young woman whose appearance was spoilt by small, near-sighted eyes behind thick spectacles. According to contemporary reports, she was lacking in sexual attraction, and had had few, if any, love affairs. She was intelligent, having studied both philosophy and psychology, and was employed as a social worker in Brooklyn, New York. Sylvia had two sisters, Hilda and Ruth; all three were members of the Socialist Workers' Party. Although Ruth had worked briefly as a secretary for the Dewey Commission, their importance in the Trotsky-

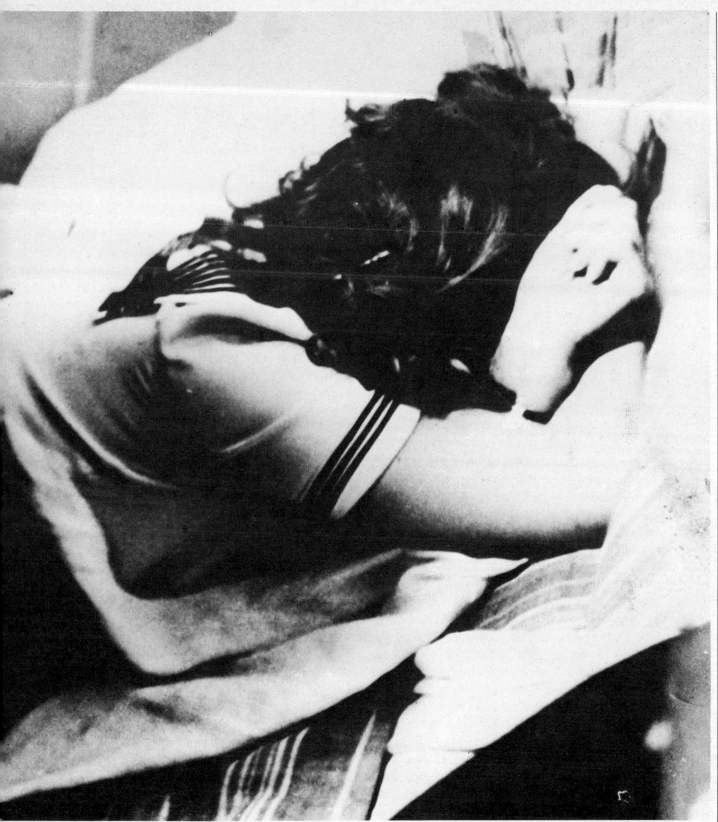

ist movement was very minor, and seems to have been overestimated by the GPU when it decided to engineer a meeting between Sylvia and its agent. The main conspirators in this elaborate plot were an American Communist, Louis Budenz; a mysterious 'Mr Roberts', later identified as Dr Gregory Rabinowitz, the American representative of the Soviet Red Cross; an even more mysterious figure known as 'Gertrude'; and Gertrude's friend Ruby Weil, who was an acquaintance of Hilda Agelof and thus provided the necessary link. Persuaded by Budenz, Roberts and Gertrude that they were 'engaged in stopping Trotsky's plottings against Stalin's life', Ruby Weil made

friends with Sylvia in New York, accompanied her on a holiday to Europe, and introduced her to a 'young student' called Mornard in Paris. The real Mornard would have been thirty-four at the time, but the bogus one was ten years younger; he was handsome, and evidently 'a man of the world', able to speak fluent Spanish and French as well as adequate English. The seduction of the inexperienced and inhibited Sylvia was an easy matter. Shortly after the start of their romance in July 1938, the headless body of Rudolf Klement, one of Trotsky's secretaries, was found floating in the Seine; at the same time, 'Mornard' told Sylvia that his mother had been injured

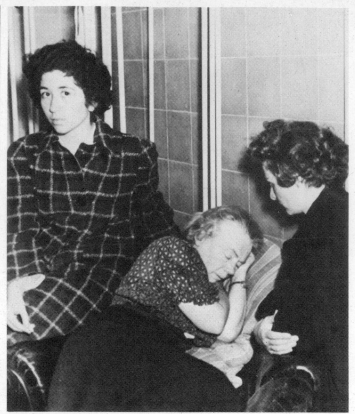

**Natalya during her ordeal at the Green Cross Hospital
Right: Sylvia Agelof is treated for shock**

in a car accident, and vanished for a few weeks. This was only one of innumerable incidents, vaguely puzzling at the time, which later acquired a sinister significance and returned to haunt Sylvia's memory after she had understood the motives that underlay 'Mornard's' courtship.

On the day of the murder, Sylvia had arranged to meet her lover at half past seven for dinner at a restaurant with Otto Schuessler. She arrived a quarter of an hour late for the appointment, and was surprised to find only Schuessler and his fiancée there. Sylvia telephoned various places where she thought Jacson might be, but it never occurred to her to ring up the Trotsky house. Schuessler finally insisted on doing so, and was told what had happened over the telephone. He broke the news to her in a taxi on the way to the Avenida Viena. She arrived there in a state of shock and was immediately taken to police headquarters, where she was arrested by Colonel Salazar who assumed that she had been an accomplice to the crime. Distraught to the verge of hysteria, she burst into tears whenever Trotsky's name was mentioned, and insisted that the police should kill her lover. When she told them that she now realized that Jacson was an agent of the GPU, they thought that she was being melodramatic and committed her to the Green Cross hospital where Trotsky lay dying and where the wounded assassin was imprisoned.

After the police had exposed the 'Mornard' story as a fabrication, they continued to interrogate the prisoner as to his real identity and motives, but could get nothing out of him. Salazar thought that a confrontation with Sylvia, whose innocence was now established, might shock him into telling the truth. Still wearing bandages round the head-wounds inflicted on him by Robins and the other guards, he was led by two policemen into a hospital room where, to his horror, he saw Sylvia lying in bed, uncontrollably sobbing. For the first time since his arrest, Jacson lost all self-control. He struggled desperately to get away, and cried out: 'Colonel, what have you done? Take me out of here!' At the sight of him, Sylvia began to scream: 'Take that murderer away! Kill him! Kill him!' Salazar begged her to talk to the man and extract the truth from him, but she refused. 'He is a hypocrite and an assassin!' she continued to shout. 'I want to see him killed the way Trotsky died. He is a *canaille*!' When Salazar asked her if it were true that Jacson had been disillusioned by Trotsky, she rounded on the murderer: 'Don't lie, traitor! Tell the truth even if you pay with your life!' Jacson was still pleading with Salazar to let him leave the room, while Sylvia could only repeat: 'Liar! Murderer! Traitor! *Canaille*!' At last the nightmarish scene came to an end; but the prisoner continued to insist that he would add nothing to the explanation given in his letter – 'even if you cut my skin off inch by inch'. From that moment he retreated into a stubborn silence, which he maintained throughout his trial and the twenty years which he was sentenced to serve in a Mexican gaol.

The assassin's identity has never been officially confirmed, but the mass of evidence which has come to light over thirty years seems to prove conclusively that his real name was Jaime Ramon Mercarder Del Rio Hernandez. Mercader was born in Barcelona on 17 February 1914, and was educated there at the English Institute and the school of the Episcopalian Fathers. His mother was always the dominating influence on his life. Caridad Hernandez Mercader was a beautiful and volatile woman who had been born in Cuba in 1892, had attended convent schools in France and Spain, and had at one time wanted to become a nun. In her nineteenth year she married Don Pablo Mercader Marina – a cautious, conservative businessman who was temperamentally her opposite. She left him in 1925, taking her five children with her to France, where she led a disorganized, Bohemian life and made three attempts to kill herself. A love affair with a Frenchman converted her to Communism; after this she became politically active in Paris, and was a close friend of many leading French Communists.

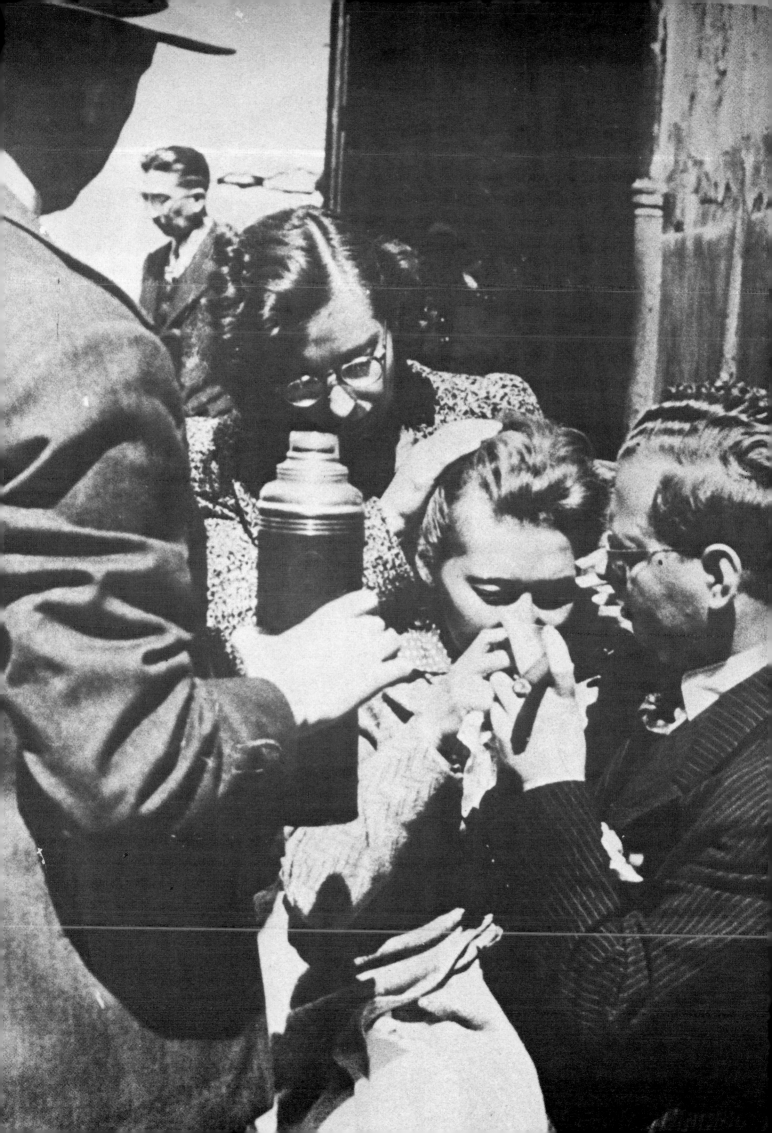

LABOR ACTION

AUGUST 26, 1940   ORGAN OF THE WORKERS PARTY, SECTION OF THE FOURTH INTERNATIONAL   THREE CE...

STALIN HAS MURDERED OUR COMRADE TROTSKY

Leon Trotsky has fallen. Our comrade, the great leader of the world revolution is dead. He was murdered at the dictate of Joseph Stalin.

Jacques Dreschd who wielded the axe that struck Trotsky is beyond any doubt a GPU agent. The last possible doubt was removed by the murderer's statement... the police that he had acted as he did because Trotsky had wanted him to commit acts of sabotage in Russia. So vile a lie could be mouthed only by the GPU.

Assigned the task of murdering Trotsky in the event that other attempts failed, Dreschd wormed his way into the household, pretending to be a "friend." The G... gave him time, time to engratiate himself, time to pretend that he had been "won over" to Trotsky's views.

The Stalinists, trying to cover the trail that can lead only to themselves, will claim that Jacques Dreschd or Monard or Jackson was a "follower" of Trotsky, ... he acted in disillusionment. So too they dared accuse Trotsky of himself organizing the May murder attempt. But Jacques Dreschd was not a follower of Trotsky. Jacq... Dreschd was a follower, and an employee, of Stalin who has levelled the muzzle of his murder machine at the man whose very life was a challenge to the Kremlin tyra...

One by one, that murder machine has struck down those closest to Trotsky, trying more desperately each time to strike at Trotsky himself.

Farewell, Leon Trotsky---

Our leader, teacher and comrade, Leon Trotsky is dead. Thus an historical epoch is ended. Lenin's co-worker and co-thinker, the leader of the October insurrection and the organizer of the once-glorious Red Army is the last of the Old Bolsheviks.

Leon Trotsky is the victim of Cain Stalin, the gravedigger of the Russian Revolution, the assassin of brave revolutionists. For almost twelve years the Kremlin oligarchies sought to take the life of Trotsky, but each time he failed. The unspeakable GPU acting through its hireling, Van Den Dreschd finally succeeded. Gaining the confidence of our warm-hearted and genial Leon Trotsky, pretending to be a disciple of our great comrade, this scoundrel in the pay of the GPU struck down the lion of October in a brutal attack. But Joseph Stalin is the real assassin—as real as if his own hand had struck the treacherous blow.

Stalin mortally feared the man whom he had driven into exile, whose comrades he murdered, whose family he destroyed. Stalin mortally feared that the deep dissatisfaction in the Soviet Union would grow to revolutionary proportions and turn to Leon Trotsky for guidance and leadership in the overthrow of his regime of terror. Stalin mortally feared that the world working-class, unfettered by the treacherous teachings of the usurpers would turn to Trotsky and the Fourth International for leadership in the struggle against reaction and for world socialism.

Stalin's hands drip with the blood of a host of fighters for proletarian emancipation. But if he thought to wipe out the revolution, he has struck in vain! If Trotsky is no more, he has left an imperishable heritage. In the period of the degeneration of the Russian Revolution, in the triumph of reactionary Stalinism, his voice and his pen remained alive to explain and to teach a new generation of young revolutionaries to fight against the decaying order of capitalism and for the new socialist society of universal freedom for the masses of our planet.

To our brave, sorrowing comrade Natalia Ivanovna, lifelong companion of Lev Davidovich, we extend our most heartfelt sympathy in this dreadful hour. You have been the comrade-in-arms of our L.D. for many decades and you have been our beloved comrade for many years. Your great devotion to your comrade and companion under the most perilous and trying conditions of the Russian revolutionary movement, in the gigantic events of the October insurrection and through the period of Stalinist degeneration and reaction, is a glorious lesson in revolutionary devotion and comradely sacrifice. Dear Natalia Ivan-

...avna, you are not alone! Thousands stand with you in this dark and bitter hour, sworn to carry on.

Leon Trotsky, the greatest disciple of Marx, Engels and Lenin, is no more. But he lives in his heroic deeds, in his great teachings! The Kremlin Borgia has finally succeeded in his villanous deed. But let him not think that thereby he has broken the living spirit of Trotsky. There are thousands now, there will be millions tomorrow who will avenge his death. They will not only avenge the murder of our dear Leon Trotsky. They will avenge the murder of the hundreds and thousands whom Stalin has destroyed in his counter-revolutionary ravages. They will march onward in the spirit of revolutionary Marxism, in the spirit of Lenin and Trotsky.

A new generation of revolutionaries is emerging. They will grow up in the spirit of Bolshevik courage and devotion to carry on until the victory of socialism. Under the banner of the Fourth International, founded by Leon Trotsky, the new movement will triumph. By his teachings, by his devotion and by his peerless courage in the face of the greatest dangers, the Fourth International will be nourished. Rising upon the edifice of the epoch of Lenin and Trotsky, it will sweep away the rubbish of the old order and give birth to the new movement of Socialist emancipation.

Farewell Leon Trotsky!

Hail the Fourth International!

Hail the liberating world revolution!

NATIONAL COMMITTEE, WORKERS PARTY
NATIONAL COUNCIL, YOUNG PEOPLES
SOCIALIST LEAGUE! (4th International)

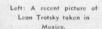

Left: A recent picture of Leon Trotsky taken in Mexico.

Below: Trotsky with several of his collaborators during the Russian Revolution.

AS THE LEADER OF THE RED ARMY

There was Blumkin, loyal soldier of the R... sian revolution. Stalin murdered him in 1929.

There was Erwin Wolff, secretary to Trot... who was kidnapped and brought to Russia in 1... by the GPU. Stalin murdered him.

There was Ignace Reiss who was found d... in Switzerland in 1937 after he had severed ... connections with the reactionary GPU. Stalin m... dered him.

There was Rudolph Klement, secretary ... Trotsky, whose mutilated body was found in ... Seine River in 1938. Stalin murdered him.

There was Sheldon Harte, bodyguard to T... sky, who was spirited away from Trotsky's ... oacan home when the GPU's May attack ta... Stalin murdered him.

There were the sons and daughters and co... less friends of Leon Trotsky. Each of them, dir... ly or indirectly, fell prey to Kremlin gangster... Only two years ago, Leon Sedov, Trotsky's ... and close collaborator, suddenly died in Paris ... der mysterious circumstances. Stalin murde... Sedov. Stalin murdered them all.

Trotsky alive was an indomitable threat to ... rotten regime of revolutionary betrayal that S... in has foisted with knout and bullet upon the R... sian masses. Each in his turn, the leaders of ... glorious revolution of 1917, that liberated ... sixth of the earth until Stalin again enslaved... have met death at the decree of Stalin. Only T... sky, organizer of the Red Army, co-worker of L... in, remained alive—a living challenge, epitom... ing the spirit of socialism and of revoluton. ... now he is dead—murdered.

For twelve years, ever since he was driven ... Stalin from the land whose rebellious forces ... led to victory in 1917, Trotsky was the targe... the GPU murder machine. They hounded ... from country to country, striking at his frie... and collaborators. And, finally, in Mexico, t... laid fine plans for the dirty business of his ... sassination. George Mink, a notorious GPU ag... was in Mexico for the express purpose of org... izing the murder. Last May they staged an arr... assault on Trotsky's home which failed in its ... only by the merest accident.

But they had reckoned with that possibil...

(Continued on page 2)

NATALIA TROTSKY
MEXICO D F

OUR HEARTS ARE TORN WITH GRIEF OVER THE LOSS WH... IS IRREPARABLY YOURS AND IRREPARABLY THAT OF IN... NATIONAL PROLETARIAN MOVEMENT. THE CAPTAIN... THE WORLD ARMY OF REVOLUTION HAS FALLEN AT ... HANDS OF THE COWARDLY ASSASSIN IN THE KREM... OUR FLAG IS DIPPED AT THE OPEN GRAVE OF THE IMM... TAL LEON TROTSKY. OUR DEEPEST SYMPATHY AND L... IS WITH YOU IN YOUR HOUR OF SORROW. LONG LIVE ... FOURTH INTERNATIONAL. LONG LIVE THE LIBERAT... TRIUMPH OF THE WORKING CLASS.

WORKERS PARTY
SHACHTMAN, SECRETA...

The front page of a Trotskyist paper, edited in New York by Max Shachtman, announced the disaster and drew correct conclusio...

e assassin — Mercader, alias Mornard, alias Jacson — bearing the wounds he received during the struggle with Trotsky's guards

At the age of fourteen, her son Ramon went to Lyons to learn the hotel business; he later worked as assistant to the chef at the Barcelona Ritz. He volunteered for military service in Spain in 1932, leaving the army two years later as a corporal. In 1935 he was arrested with other members of an underground Communist cell, and sent to a Spanish prison. When the Civil War flared up the following year, he became a political commissar, with the rank of lieutenant, in the 27th Division on the Aragon front. Caridad also enlisted, and was wounded in the shoulder; the government then sent her to Mexico at the head of a delegation of Spanish Communists. There she met Alfaro Siqueiros, whom she introduced to her son a year later when Siqueiros came to Spain to fight with the Loyalists.

On her return from Mexico, Caridad became the mistress of Leonid Eitingon, who was to prove the evil genius in her life and her son's. Under the pseudonym of General Kotov, Eitingon headed the Spanish branch of the sinister Division of Special Tasks which had recently been set up by Stalin. It was he who had master-minded the murder of Trotsky's secretary Erwin Wolf, after Wolf had left Norway for Spain in 1936, and the torture and assassination of Andres Nin, the ex-Trotskyist who led the semi-anarchist POUM (Workers' Party of Marxist Unification). Succumbing to the glamour of Eitingon's power, Caridad happily offered up Ramon as an agent. Under Eitingon's supervision, Ramon was given special training in guerrilla warfare at Barcelona; he was sent back to the front, where he received an elbow wound. He left Spain in December 1937, and reappeared in Moscow where, as Eitingon's protégé, he was instructed in the techniques of espionage and terrorism. Here, too, he first studied the files filled with details of Trotsky's habits and associates, drawn from the reports of Sobolevicius-Senin, 'Etienne' and other *agents provocateurs*. When his briefing was complete, he embarked as Mornard on the seduction of Sylvia, and as Jacson on the approach to Trotsky.

Early in 1940, Caridad followed him to Mexico City with Eitingon, who was travelling under the name of 'General Leonov'. It was later suggested that Leonov had also been the 'Felipe' who played a hidden part in the Siqueiros raid. After this had ended in fiasco, it was decided in Moscow to make another attempt on Trotsky's life, this time using different methods. Ramon suddenly left for New York in June, where he received his final instructions from Gaik Ovakimian, the permanent Resident of the GPU attached to the Soviet Consulate-General in the U.S.A. He returned to Mexico in July, and a month later the plan was put into operation. Caridad and Eitingon, in separate cars, were waiting near Trotsky's house at the time of the murder. When they saw the police arrive and realized that the assassin had been arrested, they parted and made their separate escapes from the country. They met again in Moscow some weeks later, where they had been preceded by Angelica Arenal; Siqueiros was still in hiding in Chile. Caridad was given

Left: 'Jacson' is taken into custody, with Colonel Sanchez Salazar, Chief of Police, on his left

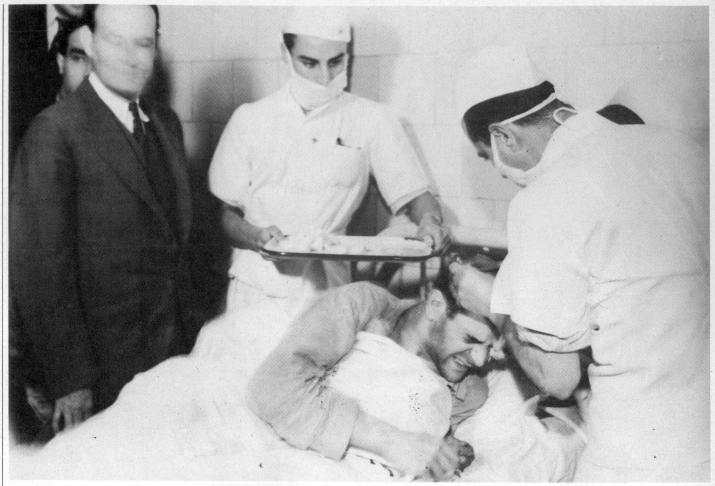

'Jacques Mornard' in Paris, 1938, with Sylvia Agelof (right) and Maria Craipeau
Above: Ramon Mercader with his mother, Caridad, during the Spanish Civil War
Top: 'Frank Jacson' in hospital after the assassination
Right: a composite made in 1950 which identifies Mercader's fingerprint in 1935 with that of Jacson-Mornard in 1940

a heroine's welcome: Beria himself presented her to Stalin, who decorated her with the Order of Lenin for her part in the murder of his enemy. Stalin also entrusted her with the Order of the Hero of the Soviet Union, which had been awarded to her son, and asked her to keep the medal in safety until it could be given to Ramon on his release from prison.

This release came on 6 May 1960. Ramon Mercader left Mexico for Cuba; from there he travelled to Prague, and it is thought that he was eventually moved to Moscow. If so, he would not have found his mother there. Caridad had soon become disillusioned in Eitingon, who turned out to have no intention of leaving his wife and children for her. Chain-smoking, unable to sleep, beginning to understand the implications of her past actions, she pestered Beria for permission to leave the Soviet Union, which she described to a friend as 'the most terrible of hells known to man'. When at last she was allowed out of Russia, she found that the long arm of the GPU still prevented her from reaching her son. She got as far as Mexico, and even to the gates of the prison where he was confined, but she never saw him; when she was nearly run over by a car, she began to suspect that she herself might be assassinated. She was last heard of in Paris, living quietly with her married daughter, an old woman tortured by grief, fear and remorse. Her former husband, Ramon's father, told an interviewer that in his opinion the Kremlin were afraid to liquidate either Caridad or her son, for fear the other might tell the whole truth at last.

A funeral service was held for Trotsky on the day after his death. In accordance with Mexican custom, a

RECCION GENERAL DE SEGURIDAD

ESPAÑA 1935	MEXICO 1940
INDICE DERECHO	INDICE DERECHO

27 26 25 24 23 22 21 20 19

27 26 25 24 23 22 21 20 19

REFERENCIAS

1 DELTA	10 CORTADA	19 ISLOTE
2 CORTADA	11 BIFURCADA	20 BIFURCADA
3 ISLOTE	12 HORQUILLA	21 CORTADA
4 FRAGMENTO	13 HORQUILLA	22 CORTADA
5 HORQUILLA	14 RAMA	23 CORTADA
6 CORTADA	15 CORTADA	24 CORTADA
7 CORTADA	16 CORTADA	25 FRAGMENTO
8 AISLADA	17 BIFURCACION	26 RAMA
9 CORTADA	18 CORTADA	27 CORTADA

1935 EN ESPAÑA
RAMON MERCADER

FOTOGRAFIA TOMADA DEL
PASAPORTE CON EL QUE

1940 EN MEXICO
"JAQUES MORNARD"

cortège marched slowly behind the coffin on its journey from the funeral parlour to the Pantheon – a distance of about eight miles. An enormous crowd followed the procession as it wound its way through the working-class districts of Mexico City. Onlookers, packing the pavements, took off their hats and stood in silence as the coffin passed them under the red flag of the Fourth International. At the Pantheon, three of the dead man's friends addressed the crowd: Albert Goldman, the lawyer who had defended Trotsky at the hearings of the Dewey Commission; Garcia Trevino, a well-known Mexican socialist; and Grandizo Munis, a leader of the Spanish wing of the Fourth International who had fought in Spain and been imprisoned there by the GPU. In Goldman's speech he assured the people of Mexico that Trotsky's remains would finally rest in the only country which had granted him asylum; but an application was made to the State Department for permission to bring the body to the U.S.A. for a second funeral service in New York. For five days it lay in state at the funeral parlour, watched over round the clock by a guard of honour composed of Mexican workers and members of Trotsky's household; about three hundred thousand people, most of them belonging to the humblest sections of the community, filed past it daily to pay their last respects.

President Cardenas and his wife paid a visit of condolence to Natalya, and assured her that they 'understood very well where letters such as that found in the assassin's clothing were manufactured'. On 26 August, the State Department of the U.S. government categorically refused to receive Trotsky's corpse: the 'planet without a visa' on which he had lived so long apparently extended its inhospitality even beyond his death. His body was cremated on the following day, and the ashes were buried in the grounds of the fortified house on the Avenida Viena. A red flag was unfurled above the white stone over the grave.

Natalya continued to live at Coyoacan with Trotsky's only surviving descendant, Seva Volkov, who was fourteen at the time of his grandfather's death. Her life there was tragically lonely – but it was made a little less so after Seva's marriage by the birth of his four daughters. In November 1954 she was invited to spend thirteen months in Paris, where many of her happiest memories were revived. A visit to New York in 1957 was less successful: when she refused to talk to a representative of the Committee on Un-American Activities, her visa was abruptly cancelled and she returned to Mexico. After the Twentieth and the Twenty-Second Congresses of the

Trotsky's coffin beneath the flag of the Fourth International
Left: Natalya at the service at the Pantheon
Overleaf: the funeral procession through Mexico City

The funeral procession enters the Pantheon
Right: Joseph Hansen (right) shields Natalya from
photographers at the funeral

Communist Party of the U.S.S.R., she applied to the
Soviet authorities for the official rehabilitation of Trotsky,
her son Lyova, and other victims of the Moscow trials.
She was not surprised to receive no reply, for she had
never believed that the 'de-Stalinization', inaugurated at
that period by a fraction of the Soviet bureaucracy, would
lead to a complete re-establishment of historic truth. In
1960 she went back to Paris where she stayed with Marguerite Bonnet, a young friend of the Rosmers; there she
died at the age of seventy-nine in January 1962. After a
funeral service, at which André Breton, Pierre Naville,
Isaac Deutscher, Joseph Hansen and other loyal friends
made speeches in her honour, her ashes were brought
home to Mexico and buried next to Trotsky's. Seva and
his family still live in the house at Coyoacan, where
Trotsky's study has been kept as it was in his lifetime.

At the age of twenty-one, exiled in Siberia, Trotsky
had proclaimed his faith in the ultimate triumph of
human reason: 'As long as I breathe, I shall fight for that
radiant future in which man will become master of the
drifting stream of his history . . .' His last public speech,
delivered at Copenhagen in 1932 under difficult and
dangerous circumstances, reaffirmed that youthful
optimism. Lecturing 'In Defence of The October Revolution', he had this to say about the future of mankind:

'Man calls himself the crown of creation. He has a
certain right to that claim. But who has asserted that
present-day man is the last and highest representative of
the species Homo sapiens? No, physically as well as
spiritually he is very far from perfection, prematurely
born biologically, with feeble thought, and has not
produced any new organic equilibrium.

'It is true that humanity has more than once brought
forth giants of thought and action who tower over their
contemporaries like summits in a chain of mountains. The
human race has a right to be proud of its Aristotle,
Shakespeare, Darwin, Beethoven, Goethe, Marx, Edison
and Lenin. But why are they so rare? Above all, because
almost without exception, they came out of the upper
and middle classes. Apart from rare exceptions, the sparks
of genius in the suppressed depths of the people are

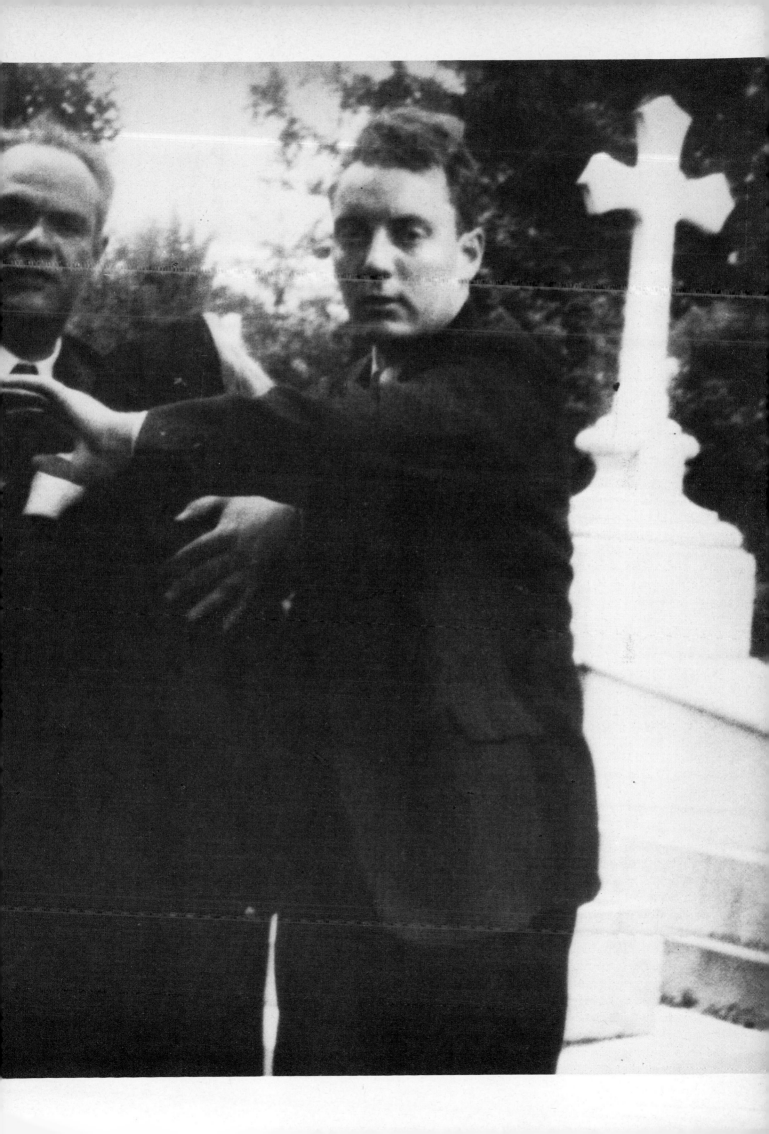

choked before they can burst into flame. But also because the processes of creating, developing and educating a human being have been and remain essentially a matter of chance, not illuminated by theory and practice, not subjected to consciousness and will.

'Anthropology, biology, physiology and psychology have accumulated mountains of material to raise up before mankind in their full scope the tasks of perfecting and developing body and spirit. Psychoanalysis, with the inspired hand of Sigmund Freud, has lifted the cover of the well which is poetically called the "soul". And what has been revealed? Our conscious thought is only a small part of the work of the dark psychic forces. Learned divers descend to the bottom of the ocean and there take photographs of the mysterious fishes. Human thought, descending to the bottom of its own psychic sources, must shed light on the most mysterious driving forces of the soul and subject them to reason and to will.

'Once he has done with the anarchic forces of his own society man will set to work on himself . . . Mankind will regard itself as raw material, or at best as a physical and psychic semi-finished product. Socialism will mean a leap from the realm of necessity into the realm of freedom in this sense also, that the man of today, with all his contradictions and lack of harmony, will open the road for a new and happier race.'

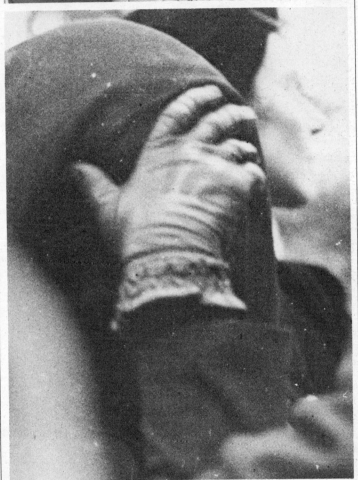

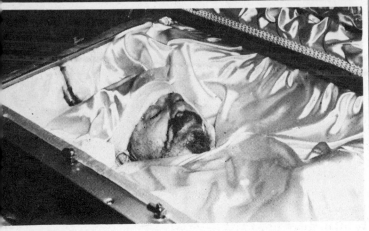

Natalya mourns
Top: Natalya watches by the coffin
Left: Trotsky in his coffin
Above left: Trotsky's coffin lies in state
Overleaf: the cremation

Testament

'For forty-three years of my conscious life I have remained a revolutionist; for forty-two of them I have fought under the banner of Marxism. If I had to begin all over again I would of course try to avoid this or that mistake, but the main course of my life would remain unchanged. I shall die a proletarian revolutionist, a Marxist, a dialectical materialist, and, consequently, an irreconcilable atheist. My faith in the communist future of mankind is not less ardent, indeed it is firmer today, than it was in the days of my youth.

'Natasha has just come up to the window from the courtyard and opened it wider so that the air may enter more freely into my room. I can see the bright green strip of grass beneath the wall, and the clear blue sky above the wall, and sunlight everywhere. Life is beautiful. Let the future generations cleanse it of all evil, oppression, and violence and enjoy it to the full.'

L. Trotsky
27 February 1940
Coyoacan

Right: the study at Coyoacan, left unchanged since Trotsky's death. Overleaf: the study window, seen from the courtyard

To Marvel and Jewell
L. T.   28/6/1940

Acknowledgements

This pictorial study of Trotsky owes an immense debt to Isaac Deutscher's definitive and monumental biography in three volumes: *The Prophet Armed, The Prophet Unarmed* and *The Prophet Outcast* (Oxford University Press, 1970, £1.25 each). The authors hope that the present book may attract further readers to Deutscher's classic work, which is not only a distinguished feat of scholarship but also an acknowledged literary masterpiece. Other books consulted include:

AVRICH, PAUL, Kronstadt 1921 *(Princeton, 1971)*

BABEL, ISAAC, Collected Stories *(Penguin, 1961)*

BONNET, MARGUERITE (ed.), Hommage à Natalia Sedova-Trotsky *(Paris, 1962)*

CARR, E. H., The Bolshevik Revolution, 1917–1923 *(three volumes, Pelican, 1966)*
    The Interregnum, 1923–1924 *(Pelican, 1969)*
    Socialism in One Country *(three volumes, Pelican, 1970)*
The Case of Leon Trotsky *(Merit, New York, 1968)*

DEUTSCHER, ISAAC, Stalin *(Pelican, 1970)*

EASTMAN, MAX, Leon Trotsky: The Portrait of a Youth *(Faber & Gwyer, 1926)*

GORKIN, JULIAN, L'Assassinat de Trotsky *(Julliard, Paris, 1970)*

HYDE, H. MONTGOMERY, Stalin *(Rupert Hart-Davis, 1971)*

LENIN, V. I., Selected Works *(three volumes, Lawrence & Wishart, 1964)*

LEVINE, ISAAC DON, The Mind of an Assassin *(Weidenfeld & Nicolson, 1959)*

ROSMER, ALFRED, Lenin's Moscow, translated by Ian H. Birchall *(Pluto Press, 1971)*

ROWSE, A. L., End of an Epoch *(Macmillan, 1947)*

SERGE, VICTOR, Memoirs of a Revolutionary, 1901–1941, translated by Peter Sedgwick *(Oxford University Press, 1963)* (with Natalya Sedova-Trotsky) Vie et Mort de Trotsky *(Paris, 1951)*

SHACHTMAN, MAX, The Bureaucratic Revolution *(Donald Press, New York, 1962)*
    Behind the Moscow Trial *(New Park Publications)*

SHUB, DAVID, Lenin *(Pelican, 1969)*

SUKHANOV, N. N. The Russian Revolution, 1917, edited Joel Carmichael *(Oxford University Press, 1955)*
The Trotsky Papers, 1917–1919 *(The Hague, 1964)*
Leon Trotsky, The Man and His Work *(Merit, 1969)*

TROTSKY, LEON, My Life, introduction by Joseph Hansen *(Pathfinder Press, New York, 1970)*
    History of the Russian Revolution, translated by Max Eastman *(three volumes, Sphere, 1967)*
    Diary in Exile, 1935, translated by Elena Zarudnaya *(Harvard University Press, 1958)*
    1905, translated by Anna Bostock *(Allen Lane The Penguin Press, 1972)*
    On Lenin: Notes Towards a Biography, translated and annotated by Tamara Deutscher, introduction by Lionel Kochan *(Harrap, 1971)*
    Stalin: An Appraisal of the Man and his Influence, translated and edited by Charles Malamuth *(two volumes, Panther, 1969)*
    The Age of Permanent Revolution: A Trotsky Anthology, edited with an introduction by Isaac Deutscher *(Dell, New York, 1964)*
    On Literature and Art, edited with an introduction by Paul N. Siegel *(Pathfinder Press, New York, 1970)*
    In Defence of Marxism *(New Park Publications, 1966)*
    The Revolution Betrayed *(New Park Publications, 1967)*
    The Permanent Revolution and Results and Prospects *(New Park Publications, 1971)*
    Writings of Leon Trotsky, 1935–1940 *(four volumes, Pathfinder Press, New York, 1970)*
    Basic Writings, edited Irving Howe *(Heinemann, 1964)*
    Essential Trotsky, edited R. T. Clark *(Allen & Unwin)*
    Literature and Revolution *(Michigan, 1960)*
    The Transitional Programme *(New Park, 1970)*
    Class and Art *(New Park Publications, 1968)*
    The Class Nature of the Soviet State *(New Park, 1968)*
    Germany 1931/2 *(New Park Publications, 1970)*
    Where is Britain Going? *(New Park Publications, 1970)*
    Lessons of October *(New Park Publications, 1971)*
    Struggle Against Fascism in Germany *(Pathfinder Press, New York, 1971)*
    Third International After Lenin *(Pathfinder Press, 1971)* (with Natalya Sedova-Trotsky) Leon Sedov: Son, Friend, Fighter *(New Park Publications, 1967)*
    In Defence of October *(New Park, 1971)*

WILDE, HARRY, Trotzki *(Rowohlt, Hamburg, 1969)*

WILSON, EDMUND, To the Finland Station *(Fontana, 1970)*

The authors express their grateful thanks to the following for their kind assistance and invaluable advice in the task of tracing the photographic material reproduced in this book: Esteban Volkov; George L. Weissman, George Breitman and Brian Shannon of the Pathfinder Press; Marguérite Bonnet; Tamara Deutscher; Jean van Heijenoort; Herman Axelbank; Sara Jacobs; Max Shachtman; Harry Wilde; Günter Dill; Julián Gorkin; Gérard Rosenthal; Gerry Healy; Michael Kettle; Professor William Rodney; Alec Flegon; Charles van Gelderen. Thanks are also due to the following organizations: Agence France-Presse; Associated Press; Beaverbrook Newspapers; the Bettman Archive, New York; Bild-Archiv Kultur und Geschichte, Munich; C. J. Bücher, Lucerne; Bund Archive, New York; Culver Pictures, New York; Eupra Press Service, Munich; Excelsior, Mexico City; Archiv Gerstenberg, Frankfurt; Granger Collection, New York; John Hillelson Agency – Magnum; Illustrationsfoto – Walter Pöppel; Institut für Politikwissenschaft der Johann-Wolfgang Goethe Universität, Frankfurt; Interfoto – Friedrich Rauch, Munich; International Instituut voor Sociale Geschiedenis, Amsterdam; Keystone Press; the Lords Gallery; Editions Minuit, Paris; New York City Public Library; Photoworld, New York; Popperfoto; Queen's University, Kingston, Ontario; Radio Times Hulton Picture Library; Collection Roger-Viollet, Paris; Len Sirman Press, Geneva; Snark International, Paris; Sovfoto, New York; Sunday Times Magazine; Tammiment Library, New York City University; Ullstein Bilderdienst, West Berlin; Underwood & Underwood, New York; United Press International. Finally, the authors wish to thank Ken Lewis for drawing the map, and Roger Volkl and Guglielmo Galvin of the Rainbow Colour Company for their excellent technical photographic assistance.

Index

Figures in bold indicate illustrations. 'T' means Trotsky